GLOBETROTTER™

KU-350-973

Travel Guide

BALTIC STATES

ROBIN AND JENNY McKELVIE

NEW
HOLLAND

NEW
HOLLAND

*** Highly recommended
 ** Recommended
  * See if you can

First edition published in 2009
by New Holland Publishers (UK) Ltd
London • Cape Town • Sydney • Auckland
10 9 8 7 6 5 4 3 2 1

website: www.newhollandpublishers.com

Garfield House, 86 Edgware Road
London W2 2EA, United Kingdom

80 McKenzie Street, Cape Town 8001
South Africa

Unit 1, 66 Gibbes Street, Chatswood
NSW 2067, Australia

218 Lake Road, Northcote
Auckland, New Zealand

Distributed in the USA by
The Globe Pequot Press, Connecticut

ISBN 978 1 84773 202 6

Publishing Manager: Thea Grobbelaar
DTP Cartographic Manager: Genené Hart
Editor: Carla Zietsman
Design and DTP: Nicole Bannister
Cartographer: Genené Hart

Picture Researcher: Shavonne Govender
Consultant: Godfrey Hall
Proofreader: Thea Grobbelaar

Reproduction by Resolution, Cape Town
Printed and bound by Times Offset (M) Sdn. Bhd.,
Malaysia.

Photographic Credits:
All pictures by **Robin McKelvie** with the exception
of the following: **Pictures Colour Library:** pages 4,
37, 50, 55, 82, 111.

Keep us Current
Information in travel guides is apt to change, which
is why we regularly update our guides. We'd be
grateful to receive feedback if you've noted something we should include in our updates. If you have
new information, please share it with us by writing to
the Publishing Manager, Globetrotter, at the office
nearest to you (addresses on this page). The most
significant contribution to each new edition will
receive a free copy of the updated guide.

Cover: *Tallinn Old Town skyline seen from
Toompea Hill.*
Title Page: *A traditional building.*

CONTENTS

3 █

1
Introducing
the Baltic States

Bordering **Poland** to the south, **Kaliningrad** to the south-west and **Belarus** to the east, Lithuania is the most southerly of the three Baltic States. It is also the largest of the Baltic countries. Although written mentions of Lithuania can be traced back more than 1000 years, it has only enjoyed independence since 1991.

By the beginning of the millennium the poorest of the Baltic States had found its feet, both economically and in terms of international tourism, welcoming 1.3 million overnight tourists and 2.9 million day-trippers in 2001. In 2005 the number of overnight tourists topped two million, with same-day visitors reaching three million.

Much of Lithuania's **recent prosperity** is attributable to its greater standing within Europe; the country (like its Baltic neighbours) was welcomed into the fold of the European Union (EU) on 1 May 2004. EU membership has been accompanied by an increase in international trade and more direct flights to Vilnius from all over Europe.

For tourists the country's biggest lure is undoubtedly its capital city. Since the early 1990s **Vilnius** has shrugged off its sleepy provincial feel and developed a cosmopolitan buzz. A forest of gleaming skyscrapers and an ever-increasing array of funky bars, modern hotels and contemporary restaurants has accompanied this new energy. Those pioneering travellers who arrived in Vilnius in the early 1990s had few choices when it came to drinking, dining and sleeping, but today the opposite is true and visitors are literally spoilt for choice.

Despite its progressive new outlook, the capital retains the old-world charms that make the city such a memorable place

LITHUANIA
TOP ATTRACTIONS

*** **Vilnius:** awash with beautiful churches, Vilnius's Old Town won't fail to impress.
*** **Curonian Spit National Park:** mesmerizing landscape of vaulting sand dunes and Baltic Sea surf.
*** **Trakai:** take a cruise or rowing boat on the lake.
** **Kaunas:** Lithuania's second city is not content to play second fiddle.
** **Nida:** this coastal settlement has been charming holiday-makers for centuries.

Opposite: *The lavish Gothic façade of the House of the Blackheads in Rīga.*

to visit. Vilnius's Baroque Old Town (which Lithuanians claim is the largest in the world) is a breathtaking showcase of vaulting church spires and Baroque architecture, which more than deserves its place on the **UNESCO World Heritage List**.

Outside the capital, Lithuania has a wealth of attractions that, in many cases, are still awaiting the arrival of tourism. Although they welcome far fewer visitors than Vilnius, the country's second city, **Kaunas** (where old and new sit side by side on the confluence of the Nemunas and Neris rivers), and the port city of **Klaipėda** are no longer tourism secrets.

Away from its cities and towns, Lithuania is blessed with 99km (62 miles) of Baltic coastline, lovingly dubbed the **Amber Coast** by the country's tourist authorities, due to the integral role of the amber trade in Lithuania's history and the fact that it remains one of its national symbols. The undisputed highlight along this expanse of white beach are the voluminous sand dunes of the **Curonian Spit** (another of Lithuania's UNESCO World Heritage Sites).

Inland Lithuania boasts almost 22,000km² (8494 sq miles) of **lush green forest** (covering a third of the country's landmass) and a seemingly infinite number of **sparkling lakes** and **meandering rivers**, some of which are protected in **five national** and **30 regional parks**. It is perfect for outdoor activities that encompass everything from canoeing to mountain biking.

For those who prefer their relaxation to take a more sedentary form, healing mineral waters and pampering massages are on hand in **spa towns** like **Druskininkai**. The current trend for spa tourism means that the resorts are starting to enjoy the same level of popularity that they did when they opened in the 19th century.

In a country celebrating more than ten centuries of history, those who want to revive ancient customs can see colourful **folk performances**, or listen to traditional Lithuanian music. Highlights on Lithuania's cultural calendar include the Vilnius Festival (June–July), Pažaislis Festival (July–August) and the Kristupo Vasaros (July–August).

The middle of the Baltic States sandwich, **Latvia**, is larger than its northern Estonian neighbour, but smaller than Lithuania to the south. Like its Baltic siblings this **fledgling**

nation has only enjoyed full independence since 1991. Until the
country's 2004 accession to the EU,
many prospective visitors would (if
they were honest) have been hard
pushed to place Latvia on the map.
The 'open skies policy' of aviation
liberalization that accompanied its
EU membership, though, has seen
the number of flights to the capital,
Rīga, increase dramatically and the
cost of travelling to Latvia plummet.
More frequent and affordable access,
global media coverage and word of mouth have in turn
helped place the country firmly on the tourism map.

Above: *Rīga's Old Town
these days is covered with
cafés, bars and restaurants
– a far cry from the days
of communist-era
deprivations.*

One downside of this can be the weekend invasion of
groups of men (often stag parties celebrating an impending
marriage) from Britain, who arrive in Rīga in search of
cheap alcohol and nefarious nights out. Fortunately the
city is big enough to accommodate everyone.

The **most cosmopolitan** of the Baltic capitals, Rīga has
established itself as a destination that combines historical
sights (as showcased in its UNESCO World Heritage listed
Old Town) and a raucous nightlife scene. For the discern-
ing traveller it also offers **top-notch hotels**, **first-rate
restaurants** and a **raft of cultural attractions**. While the
majority of foreigners visiting Latvia enjoy a city break in
the capital, the country's myriad other attractions are also
beginning to move into the limelight.

Latvia's bustling port cities of **Liepāja** and **Ventspils** have
benefited from recent investment in their tourism infrastructure. The combination of award-winning beaches, communist history, traditional timber-framed buildings and a
clutch of churches ensure their enduring popularity with
the domestic market, with international visitors also filter-
ing through in ever greater numbers.

For those who prefer to take their holidays at a more
tranquil pace, Latvia also boasts 12th- and 13th-century
settlements like **Ludza**, **Cēsis** and **Kuldīga**, where on quiet
afternoons it often feels as if the hands of time stopped tick-

LATVIA TOP ATTRACTIONS

*** Rīga: the city's architectural heritage has more
than earned it its status as a
UNESCO World Heritage
Site.
*** Cape Kolka: this
windswept point, where
the Gulf of Rīga and Baltic
Sea collide, is the most
impressive stretch of Latvia's
coastline.
*** Cēsis: its dramatic ruined
castle is just one of this
ancient town's impressive
sights.
*** Kuldīga: one of Latvia's
oldest and prettiest towns.
*** Rūndale Palace: the most
ornate stately home in the
Baltic States.

ing hundreds of years ago. Then there are opulent palaces and dramatic fortresses. No visit to the country is complete without checking out Francesco Bartolomeo Rastrelli's ornate masterpiece, **Rundāle Palace**. The bustling Zemgale town of **Jelgava** and the tranquil countryside around **Mežotne** also boast their own handsome country houses.

When it comes to ancient fortifications it often feels as if these are located at every turn. You can't travel far in Latvia without coming across a **dramatic castle**, impressive **ruins** or an **ancient mound**. Those at Kuldīga, Bauska and Ludza are amongst the most dramatic.

For many repeat visitors, though, there is only one reason for travelling to and within Latvia, and that is to spend time **getting active** in a seemingly endless expanse of **unspoiled countryside**. Few visitors are aware that this compact Baltic State boasts a **wild** and **rugged coastline** that unfurls over 531km (330 miles), where surf rolls onto broad stretches of deserted golden sand. Even in the height of summer, when the water is relatively tame and locals spend long, lazy summer days soaking up the sun's rays, you never have to look too hard to find your own private stretch of beach.

Away from its **vast beaches**, Latvia will also impress visitors with gushing rivers, lush fields, vast trackts of native forest, undulating hills and vast lakes. A haven for **outdoor enthusiasts**, the countryside provides opportunities for doing everything from horse riding, cycling and kayaking to bungee jumping and skiing. One of the greatest pleasures in rural Latvia is staying in a secluded lakeside log cabin where, as you take a dip in the cool water before cosying up in front of the wood-burning stove, it feels as if the modern world is very far away indeed.

Whether you are looking for the type of gastronomic experience that can be found in Rīga, and encompasses everything from traditional Latvian theme restaurants to funky bistros and world cuisine, the throbbing nightlife of the capital, folk performances, a seaside holiday, a tranquil rural break or a heart-stopping white-knuckle adventure, this small Baltic country has something to suit everyone.

The most northerly of the Baltic States, **Estonia** shares land borders with **Latvia** to the south and **Russia** to the east. While Estonia has a rich history, it has, with the exception of the interwar period (1920–40) only been an independent country since 1991, when its status was accepted by the international community.

Estonia is culturally and linguistically very different to the other Baltic countries, having more in common with its Scandinavian brethren in the north (reserve and efficiency being amongst the country's key traits) than its generally more impulsive neighbours in the south.

Estonia is also more **economically prosperous** than Latvia and Lithuania. Tourism makes a significant contribution to the country's financial wellbeing, and arrivals figures (around 1.5 million foreign tourists and almost a million domestic holiday-makers) make happy reading for anyone with a vested interest in the industry. The recent **growth in tourism** and the wider economic health of the country are in part attributable to Estonia's entrance into the fold of the European Union. Like Latvia and Lithuania it became a full member of the EU in 2004. It also joined NATO that year.

In common with its southern neighbours, the majority of overseas visitors to Estonia simply take a city break in the capital. Tallinn's stunning **medieval Old Town** is one of the most attractive in Europe, where vaulting church spires, sturdy old fortifications and the grand merchant houses which line its cobbled streets all vie for a view over the Baltic Sea. Old-world boutique hotels, a handful of excellent restaurants and a wealth of lively cafés and bars complement Tallinn's physical charms. To end your exploration of Estonia here, though, sells the country short.

Visitors from Finland and Sweden, as well as the Estonians themselves, have long been aware of the myriad attractions of the country's **expansive coastline**. **Sandy beaches** and **therapeutic spas** have always been the primary attraction of **Pärnu**; in a bid to broaden its appeal to

---

*** **Tallinn:** another very deserving UNESCO World Heritage listed architectural gem.
*** **Pärnu:** feel the stresses and strains of 21st-century life ease away as you indulge in a pampering spa treatment and admire the city's eclectic architecture.
*** **Lahemaa National Park:** dotted with erratic boulders and rolling dunes, this coastal conservation area is a winner.
*** **Saaremaa:** get away from it all on Estonia's biggest island.
*** **Tartu:** party with the local students in the country's second city.

Opposite: *Cycling around the Old Town walls with their fortifications and watchtowers, just one of the ways to explore the Estonian capital's historic old core.*

Area: 45,227km² (17,462 sq miles)
Location: Estonia shares land borders with Latvia in the south and Russia in the east. The Baltic Sea lies to the north (the Gulf of Finland) and the west.
Coastline: Estonia's coastline (including that of its islands) measures 3794km (2357 miles).
Language: Estonian
Population: 1,340,000
Religion: Majority Lutheran
Currency: Estonian *kroon* and *senti* (100 *senti* = 1 *kroon*).
Government: Parliamentary Democracy

international visitors the standard of accommodation available has also improved in recent years. Warmer summer sea temperatures, a dramatic semi-ruined castle and a handful of museums have also put **Haapsalu** on the domestic tourism map, with those from overseas slowly discovering its charms.

Some of the most undiscovered areas of Estonia are its **islands**. Saaremaa, the biggest in the country, combines old-world charm, historic sights, unspoiled nature and a laid-back way of life.

Estonia's appeal is by no means confined to its shoreline, with the ancient university city of **Tartu**, located on the banks of the Emajögi River, impressing visitors with its attractive architecture and lively atmosphere. **Ancient fortifications** and a rich and **diverse nature** (much of it protected within nature reserves and national parks) that incorporates vast tracts of woodland, boggy wetlands, vast lakes, gushing rivers and hills high enough for skiing help complete the picture. Then there is the country's **rich cultural heritage**, perhaps best explored in its old towns and the unique Setu culture that still exists in Setumaa in the very southeastern corner of the country. For those whose ideal holidays involve getting in and about the countryside, then Estonia's natural environment also lends itself to a broad sweep of **outdoor activities** including sailing, fishing, snowboarding, hiking, cycling, canoeing and climbing.

THE LAND
Lithuania

Spanning **65,300km²** (25,212 sq miles), Lithuania is a small country located in northeastern Europe. It shares 1747km (1086 miles) of land borders with Belarus, Kaliningrad, Latvia and Poland.

The country is loosely divided between the **Aukštaitija** (Highlands) and the **Žemaitija** (Lowlands) and more formally into **ten counties**: Alytus, Marijampolė, Kaunas, Klaipėda, Panevėžys, Šiauliai, Telšiai, Tauragė, Utena and Vilnius. These counties are then subdivided into smaller local regions.

Lithuania is the **largest** of the Baltic States (just slightly larger than Ireland in both land area and population). The country's **geology** is reasonably diverse with fertile plains, dense forests, rolling hills, a flurry of lakes, marshes, powerful rivers and a small stretch (99km/62 miles) of Baltic Sea coastline. These habitats are home to a large number of **animals** and **insects**, including beavers, wild boars and lynxes, although you are more likely to see foxes, hedgehogs and deer. Around 300 types of **bird** also make the most of Latvia's natural landscape, with boggy wetlands proving ideal breeding and nesting grounds for them. Lithuania's **coastal waters** meanwhile are home to myriad varieties of marine life, including dolphins, salmon and cod.

Above: *Latvia's windswept and amber-strewn Baltic coastline is one of the country's key attractions with mile upon mile of unspoiled sandy beach.*

Lithuania's main tourist drawcards are its cities, leaving the bountiful **national parks**, **nature reserves**, **lakes** and **rivers** to the locals and adventurous visitors. In total there are five national parks and four nature reserves, with the highlights **Aukštaitija National Park**, **Dzūkija National Park** and **Žemaitija National Park**.

Lithuania has a relatively mild climate given its northerly location, and this is primarily due to the influence of the Gulf Stream, which means that the coast tends to enjoy milder weather than the continental east of the country. Summer days (June–September) are warm – the mercury generally exceeds 15ºC (59ºF), reaching the mid-20s in July and August. Late May and early October are also comparatively mild. Winters (November–March) are long and cold, with average temperatures below 0ºC (32ºF) in all areas of the country.

Latvia

Spanning just **64,589km²** (24,938 sq miles), Latvia is a small country located in northeastern Europe. It shares land borders with Lithuania, Belarus, Russia and Estonia.

The country is divided into five broad **regions**: Rīga, Kurzeme, Zemgale, Vidzeme and Latgale. In turn these are subdivided into 26 **administrative districts**, which com-

CLIMATE

Lithuania, Latvia and Estonia all have temperate climates. Summers are reasonably warm, springs and autumns mild (particularly May and September). Long winters last from November through to the middle of March and can be very cold, with daytime temperatures often falling below 0ºC (32ºF). Heavy snowfall, ice and frost are common at this time. It is generally slightly warmer on the coast. It rains throughout the year, with August the wettest month.

CHANGING FROM RED TO GREEN

Environmental issues were not exactly given much attention by the Soviet authorities and all three countries are still coming to terms with this polluted legacy. There are hulking old-fashioned power plants and swathes of now often defunct heavy industrial developments, as well as rivers and lakes that have suffered years of serious pollution. Things have changed since 1991 and now serious attempts are being made to shift from a red to a green mindset.

Below: *The River Gauja is at the heart of the very popular Gauja National Park, a favourite with everyone from Latvian families who wants to relax at the weekend through to tourists wanting to enjoy the adventure sports on offer.*

prise 453 *pagasts* (civil parishes) and 70 towns. In addition, Latvia has a number of **cities**, including: Rīga, Daugavpils, Liepāja, Jelgava, Jūrmala, Ventspils and Rēzekne.

Despite its small size, Latvia boasts a varied **geology** with fertile plains, a lengthy coastline, dense forests, rolling hills, great lakes, marshland and powerful rivers all part of the mix. Like neighbouring Lithuania these diverse habitats are home to well in excess of 1000 species of **fauna**, including beavers, wild boars, lynxes, foxes, hedgehogs and deer. **Birds** also make the most of Latvia's natural landscape, with boggy wetlands providing ideal breeding and nesting grounds. Latvia's **coastal waters** meanwhile are home to many varieties of marine life, including dolphins and grey seals.

Latvia's tourist industry is largely centred around its cities and coast; this means that the country's **national parks**, **nature reserves**, **lakes** and **rivers** are often overlooked. Latvia's most famous national park is the **Gauja National Park** (*see* fact panel, page 89), of which the eponymous **Gauja River** (one of Latvia's longest at 452km/281 miles) is an integral part.

Latvia has a transitional **climate** (between the maritime climate of the west and Russia's continental climate to the east). Summer days (June–September) are warm – average temperatures generally exceed 15°C (59°F), reaching the mid-20s on July and August days. Late May and early October are also comparatively mild. Winters (November–March) are long and cold, with average temperatures in Rīga reaching just -3°C (26°F) in January and often staying as low as 5°C (41°F) in April.

Estonia
Spanning just **45,227km²** (17,462 sq miles) Estonia is by far the **smallest** of the Baltic States, though it features perhaps the most wide-ranging geography. It shares land borders with only Russia and Latvia, though it is just a short hop across the Baltic Sea from Helsinki in Finland.

The main administrative delineation in Estonia is between counties. The country is subdivided into a number of **counties**: Tallinn, Harju, Hiiu, Ida-Viru, Jõgeva, Järva, Lääne, Lääne-Viru, Põlva, Pärnu, Rapla, Saare, Tartu, Valga, Viljandi and Võru.

Despite being one of the most compact countries in Europe, Estonia boasts an impressively diverse **geology** with fertile plains, a lengthy coastline laden with sandy beaches, dense forests, rolling hills, great lakes and marshy wetlands. These myriad habitats are home to well in excess of 1000 varieties of insects and animals, including lynxes, wild boars, beavers, deer, hedgehogs and foxes. A variety of birds also make the most of Estonia's natural landscape, with its wetlands proving ideal breeding and nesting grounds. Estonia's **coastal waters** meanwhile are home to myriad varieties of marine life.

Like Latvia, Estonia's tourist industry is focused on its cities and coast; this means that the country's natural attractions, preserved in **national parks** and **nature reserves**, are largely unexplored. Three of the country's four national parks were established after independence as attempts were made to reverse decades of Soviet ecological damage. Perhaps the most accessible and rewarding park for visitors is **Lahemaa National Park**. Estonia also boasts over 1500 islands, a sprinkling of which are accessible by boat.

Given its northerly location, Estonia has a milder **climate** than you might expect due to the influence of the Gulf Stream. Summer days (June–September) are warm, with daytime temperatures regularly reaching the early to mid-20s. Late May and early October are also comparatively mild. Winters (November–March) are long and cold, with average temperatures across the country staying below 0ºC (32ºF).

HISTORY IN BRIEF
Lithuanian History
Just how long Lithuanians have been settled on Lithuanian territory is contested amongst historians, with some dating their arrival back to 2500BC and others to the 1st century AD, though the first human settlers may have appeared as

VILSANDI NATIONAL PARK

This unusual national park spreads its protective wings over 10% of all Estonia's islands. Although the national park was only declared in 1993, the area was the first ever protected nature reserve in the Baltics as far back as the start of the 20th century. The national park encompasses Vilsandi Island, the western coast of Saaremaa and around 160 small islets with a total area of 182km² (70 sq miles). Over 250 bird species are found in the park with over 100 breeding here.

early as 10,000BC. What is agreed, though, is that the **first written reference** to Lithuania occurred in 1009.

Lithuania's history has been a turbulent one, marked by a string of attacks and invasions by foreign powers. Over the centuries everyone – from **medieval Russia** and **Prussian Lords** to the **Teutonic Knights** (from Germany), **Nazi Germany** and the **Russian communists** – has fought for control of Lithuanian soil.

However, the country has not always been a victim. During the 14th century the **Jogailan Dukes** ruled an empire that extended from the Baltic to the Black Sea. The coronation of Jogaila, who became Władysław II Jogaila, King of Poland, enhanced Jogailan power, and the birth of Jogaila's son, Casimir IV, saw the allegiance between Lithuania and Poland last until the late 18th century and the partition of Poland.

By **1795** the bulk of Lithuania had been subsumed into Russia, save a token section that fell under Prussian control. Russia's dominion didn't sit easily with the Lithuanian people, who protested at intervals throughout the 19th century and again in the early 20th century.

World War I temporarily heralded the end of Russian rule in Lithuania, and the country fell under the auspices of Germany. At the end of the war the Lithuanians wasted no time in asserting their independence, and the country remained autonomous until 1939 and the outbreak of **World War II**. Fear of Nazi designs on Klaipėda (Memel in German) saw a desperate Lithuania sign an agreement of mutual assistance with the Soviet government in October that year. This move effectively sounded the death knell for independence. Eight months later Lithuania had a communist pro-Soviet government, political dissenters were banished and in July 1940 there was a vote to integrate Lithuania into **Russia**.

The country's transition into expansionist Russia did not run smoothly. In the first instance a number of countries, including the USA, disputed the legality of such a move. Then, as German forces advanced on Russia, **anti-Russian protests** broke out all over Lithuania as the Russians were forced to retreat.

German occupation, though, proved to be equally horrific for the Lithuanian people. The invading Nazi troops methodically sacked the country, murdering and raping thousands as they went. It is estimated that up to a quarter of a million Lithuanians were exterminated between 1940 and 1944; many of them Jewish.

The assertion of **Soviet** control at the end of World War II didn't bring an end to the atrocities suffered by the Lithuanians. Instead it heralded a period of **mass deportations** to Siberian labour camps (historians put the number of exiles at around 350,000), with liberals, intellectuals and opponents of the communist regime all displaced. In the **postwar years** the Soviet government imposed a strict communist regime on the country. Its most draconian measures included the forced closure of churches, the banning of religious icons and the expulsion of priests. As thousands of Lithuanians were dispatched to Siberia, workers from Poland and Russia were shipped in.

By the late 1980s the desire for **self-rule** was beating strong and, taking its lead from the political changes in other Eastern European countries, Lithuania proclaimed itself independent on 11 March 1990. As tensions mounted military reprisals followed in 1991, leaving over 100 people wounded and 21 dead in two separate incidents.

The **crumbling USSR**, however, was unable to keep control and officially acknowledged the new and autonomous **Republic of Lithuania** on 6 September 1991. In the same month Lithuania joined the United Nations (UN). The next big year in the country's history came in **2004** when it joined both **NATO** and the **European Union** (EU).

Latvian History

Latvia was first inhabited as early as 10,000BC. A key period in the country's history came around 2000BC when **Baltic tribes** (Livs, Selonians, Latgallians, Couronians and Semgallians) settled along the coast. Much of Latvia's **documented history**, though, dates from the late 12th century. This period, until the outbreak of war in 1914, saw the territory come under **German**, **Swedish**, **Polish** and **Russian** rule.

LITHUANIA HISTORICAL CALENDAR

10th century BC Evidence of early settlement in Lithuania.
AD1009 First written mention of the country.
1323 Grand Duke Gediminas establishes Vilnius.
1386 Unification of Lithuania and Poland through marriage.
15th century Establishment of Jewish culture in Lithuania.
1569 Lithuanian-Polish commonwealth.
1795 Russian rule comes to Lithuania.
1860–85 National awakening/Lithuanian uprising.
1918 Declaration of independence.
1939 USSR occupies Lithuania.
1941 Nazi Germany occupation.
1944 Russian occupation.
1990 Declaration of independence.
1991 Lithuanian independence recognized.
2004 Lithuania joins the EU and NATO.

Key events during those 700 years included the advent of Christianity (in the late 12th to early 13th century), the establishment of the **Livonian State** in 1270, the late 13th-century ascension of Rīga and Cēsis (amongst other Latvian places) to the **Hanseatic League**, the **Livonian Wars** (1558–83), the Polish conquest of Latgale (1561–1772) and the Swedish occupation of Vidzeme and Rīga (1621–1710). Both Polish and Swedish territory later fell under Russian control, with the rest of Latvia following suit by the close of the 18th century.

The second half of the 18th century was characterized by the pursuit of a **national identity**. During this time the Bible was translated into Latvian for the first time and Rīga gained its first theatre. Latvian identity went from strength to strength throughout the 19th and 20th centuries, with the publication of Latvian newspapers, the establishment of the **'Latvian Awakening'** movement (1873), the setting up of Latvia's first political party (the Latvian Social Democratic Workers' Party) in 1904 and a general strike, later dubbed the **Latvian Revolution**, in 1905.

Latvia emerged from the rubble of World War I as an annexe to Russia. The Latvians then became embroiled in a two-year battle for independence with the occupying forces.

The remainder of the country's inter-war period (1920–39) was marked by economic depression and political unrest. Four years before the outbreak of **World War II** the Freedom Monument was erected in Rīga (*see page 65*). Even today it is an enduring symbol of the nation's desire for autonomy. After spending the war alternately dominated by Germany and Russia, Latvia became part of the **Soviet Union** for over four decades (1944–91).

Russian leadership, though, didn't go unchallenged, with rebels battling for independence until 1956 (some of the Forest Brothers fought on long after), and **political demonstrations** breaking out in 1988. A year later Latvia held its first democratic election. The most momentous event in the country's history, however, was the vote for and the achievement of **independence** in 1991.

For many Latvians the eventual price of self-rule was high. During more than four decades of Soviet rule thousands of intellectuals and dissidents were **deported**, murdered or simply disappeared, with those who were **exiled** to Siberia amongst the lucky ones.

In May 1990 Latvia declared itself independent. In a desperate bid to keep Latvia within the Soviet Union, President **Gorbachev** unleashed his special forces on Rīga, and on 20 January 1991 they shot into a crowd of demonstrators, killing five. Today, the city's Bastejkalns Park (see page 66) contains poignant reminders of that fateful evening. Latvians, however, were not deterred and in a referendum held in March 1991 the majority of Latvians (74%) voted for autonomy.

Trouble brewed again in Moscow with the **attempted coup** on 19 August 1991. Ultimately events in the Russian capital took precedence, with the disastrous rebellion against Gorbachev forcing the Russian leader to concentrate on events closer to home. The Soviet Union officially recognized the independent **Republic of Latvia** on 6 September 1991, four days after the USA did.

Since achieving self-rule, Latvia has joined the **United Nations** (1991), **NATO** (2004) and the **EU** (2004).

Above: *The Changing of the Guard ceremony at the Freedom Monument in Rīga is a symbol of the new Latvia and a reminder of darker days.*

Estonian History

Estonia's human history dates back to 10,000BC, when the first settlers set up home on its Baltic coast. These **early settlers** lived a simple life farming the land and fishing the country's coastal waters. At the beginning of the 9th century AD Estonia was invaded by Vikings; this act sparked 300 years of **Viking raids** around the Baltic, many of which were conducted by Estonian Vikings.

By the middle of the **11th century** Estonia had become a target for Russian aggression, although the sporadic attacks that spanned the next 150 years were largely unsuccessful. In 1219 Estonia's luck ran out as **Denmark** seized control of the north of the country. Just eight years later the rest fell under **German control**. In the middle of the 14th century the Danes sold their territory to German

Not content to see their nations subjugated under Soviet rule, bands of men took to the forests of all three Baltic nations following the Russian occupation at the end of World War II. They fought bitter guerrilla skirmishes against Soviet troops with their bravery unfortunately often resulting in reprisals against the local people. The last of the Forest Brothers evaded the might of the Red Army until as late as the 1980s.

10th century BC Early settlers.
8th–11th century AD Viking raids.
1219 Danish occupation of northern Estonia.
1227 German crusades.
1346 Teutonic Knights take over parts of northern Estonia.
1525 First Estonian-language book printed.
1561 Swedish invasion.
1710 Russian occupation.
Mid-19th century National awakening.
1918 Declaration of independence.
1920–40 Two decades of autonomy.
1940 Red Army troops occupy Estonia.
1941 Nazi German conquest.
1944 Russians return to power.
1991 Independence officially recognized.
2004 NATO and EU membership.

Teutonic Knights who in turn sold it on to Livonian Knights. These moves helped ensure that Germans (who comprised a sizeable minority) held considerable sway over the country for seven centuries.

Estonia's status quo was disrupted once again in 1561 when the country was conquered by **Sweden**. Their dominion was to last just 149 years, with the Russians seizing the territory in 1710 (this time the invading power was happy to leave the Germans in charge at a local level). **Russian victory** came at an incredibly high price for those living in Tallinn: around 80,000 people died (around 80% of the population) from either hunger or the plague.

In the background to these momentous shifts in power was a gradual awakening of an **Estonian national consciousness**. Key events included the publication of the first Estonian-language book in 1525 and the 1793 translation of the Bible into Estonian. By the 1880s the Russians had grown so worried by the strength of national feeling within the country that they embarked upon a period of intense **Russification**. Forcing Estonians to speak Russian when conducting official business, installing Russians in political office and other key administrative roles and the influx of more Russian nationals were amongst the reactionary measures taken by the authorities. These actions, though, only served to fuel the popular discontent, and in 1905 nationwide **anti-Russian demonstrations**, like those in neighbouring Latvia and Lithuania, broke out.

At the end of **World War I**, Estonia, like its Baltic State siblings, declared itself independent, and this autonomy was finally ceded in 1920. **World War II** signalled the end of Estonian self-rule, with the country passing between **Nazi Germany** and **Soviet Russia** before being completely absorbed within the **USSR** in 1944.

The next 50 years were harsh ones, with mass deportations to Siberia and the flight of thousands of refugees both characteristic of the earlier years. Although the political scene settled down many Estonians were far from happy under the new regime, which effectively isolated the country by banning Westerners until 1960 and even then severely restricting their movements. Again, in line with protests in

Latvia and Lithuania, the first overt demonstrations against Soviet rule were staged in 1987. Demonstrations continued over the next three years, in a period dubbed the **Singing Revolution** due to the fact that protestors often sang in Estonia. In an impressive act of defiance around 500,000 Estonians (approximately a third of the country's population) attended the 1990 Song Festival (the first conducted in Estonian since the war). Then in March 1991 the majority of Estonians voted to become independent once again.

Again it was the failed coup at the Kremlin in the summer of 1991 which spared Estonia from feeling the might of the Soviet army and the battle for independence was won. The autonomous **Republic of Estonia** was officially recognized by Russia on 6 September 1991.

In 2004 Estonia's integration into Europe was finalized when its was admitted into both **NATO** and the **EU**.

GOVERNMENT AND ECONOMY
Lithuanian Government and Economy

After officially breaking free from the shackles of the USSR on 6 September 1991, the independent **Republic of Lithuania** implemented its own democratic constitution on 25 October 1992. The legislative and judicial branches of government operate independently. The former is concerned with the day-to-day running of the country and the latter with law and order.

There are 141 seats in the Lithuanian **Seimas** (parliament) and elected members of parliament (50% are selected by proportional representation, the other 50% by direct vote) sit for four years. All **Lithuanian citizens** aged 18 years or over are eligible to vote.

In addition to the prime minister, who is at the helm of the country, Lithuania also has a president; Gediminas Vagnorius and Vytautas Landsbergis were the first people to hold these respective positions after independence. In 2007 Gediminas Kirkilas was prime minister and Valdas Adamkus president.

Lithuania's leading **political parties** include the **Social Democrats**, the **Labour Party**, the

Below: *The Lithuanian flag.*

When the Russians fled following independence they left Lithuania with one hulking great problem. The nuclear power plant at Ignalina features reactors of the same design as that which exploded at Chernobyl. In recent years the EU has intervened to encourage the Lithuanians to close the twin reactors for good, with an accompanying raft of financial guarantees as the plant still supplies the majority of the country's power needs.

Conservative Party, the **New Union**, the **Liberal Centre Union** and the **Liberal Democratic Party**.

Historically Lithuania had an agricultural economy, but the end of World War II marked a gradual change that eventually saw industry become increasingly important to the country's financial health. Under the **USSR** Lithuania's economic growth was sluggish due to policies that provided the working population with jobs for life and gave the state control over everything from factories to hotels.

Major **economic change** accompanied Lithuania's 1991 independence, with the most radical reforms bringing **mass privatization** and the active encouragement of **foreign investment**. While this has not been without problems it has brought greater prosperity to the country, which has enjoyed **steady economic growth** in recent years. In 2006 alone Lithuania's Gross Domestic Product (GDP) grew by around 7.5%. Both foreign investment and opportunities for international trade have increased significantly since Lithuania joined the EU in 2004.

Today, service industries (including tourism) make the biggest contribution to Lithuania's **GDP**, although agriculture, forestry and industry all remain important.

Latvian Government and Economy

Like Lithuania, Latvia has separate legislative and judicial bodies. Parliamentary decisions are made in the **Saeima** (parliament), whose 100 members are democratically elected every four years. Both the country's prime minister and its president also stand for election every four years. To be eligible to vote you must be 18 years old or more and a citizen of the country. This latter requirement is a source of controversy due to Latvia's sizeable Russian minority (around 25% of the population). Approximately two-thirds of this group do not have citizenship due to language barriers, failure to pass Latvian history tests, or simple refusal to kowtow to what they deem unreasonable demands.

Following Latvia's 1991 declaration of independence, Ivars Godmanis became the country's first prime minister. Aigars Kalvitis

Below: *The Latvian flag.*

and Valdis Zatlers currently hold the respective offices of prime minister and president.

Latvian political parties number around 15, with the **People's Party**, the **New Era Party**, the **First Party**, **Human Rights in a United Latvia**, **Union for the Fatherland and Freedom** and the **Alliance of the Greens and Farmers Union** among the most influential.

Above: *The Estonian flag.*

Decades of **Soviet rule** and neglect left the Latvian economy in a weak state. The most pessimistic of analysts predicted that, as its trade links with Russia were eroded, the economy of an independent Latvia would simply fail.

Fortunately these forecasts were way off the mark and Latvia today boasts a **booming market economy** with Russia remaining its biggest commercial partner. Traditional industries like agriculture, manufacturing and shipbuilding remain integral to the country's economic success, but tourism and new technologies are becoming increasingly important.

Latvia's 2004 membership of the **European Union** provided another welcome boost to the national economy, with greater levels of foreign investment accompanying the rapid growth in tourism and expanded trade opportunities (especially with the UK, Sweden and Germany). Riga is currently trying to establish itself as the business hub of the Baltic States.

Estonian Government and Economy

Estonia's parliamentary system is broadly similar to those of Lithuania and Latvia. The country's executive, which co-ordinates the daily running of Estonia, is led by the prime minister. Prime Minister Andrus Ansip was re-elected in April 2007. His government is a coalition between three **political parties**: the Estonian Reform Party, the Union of Pro Patria and Res Publica and the Estonian Social Democratic Party.

The Estonian parliament is called the **Riigikogu** (National Council) and it has 101 members. Although it has been sitting under various regimes for almost 90 years, the first elections of the Democratic Republic of Estonia were not held until 1992, months after the country regained its independence. Elections are held every four years and any Estonian citizen over the age of 18 is allowed to vote. Members of

LATVIA SCARED EUROVISION VICTORY

Cynics be wary of deriding the cheesiness of the Eurovision Song Contest in this part of the world. Estonia became the first Baltic country to win with Tanel Padar and Dave Benton's duet *Everybody* in 2001, a win that was greeted with wild celebrations. Tallinn proudly held the event the following year and, lo and behold, Latvia triumphed with Marija Naumova's bubbly *I Wanna*. She fought off a tough challenge from Malta with the casting vote coming from – you guessed it – Lithuania.

Konstantin Päts (his surname refers to a type of Estonian bread) was the first ever president of an independent Estonia. Born in Estonia in 1874 (he died in 1956), he enjoyed a colourful life serving as a soldier in the Russian army, a newspaper editor and as the deputy mayor of Tallinn, as well as enjoying such eclectic hobbies as translating and beekeeping. He led the country for five separate periods between 1921 and 1937.

parliament are elected from 12 administrative regions. Many visitors to Estonia see the country's seat of power, situated within Tallinn's Toompea Castle, without realizing it.

Like its Baltic State siblings, Estonia also has a **president**. At the start of 2008 the country's head of state was President Toomas Hendrik Ilves.

By no means a poor 'Eastern European country', Estonia enjoys a higher **GNI per capita** than both Latvia and Lithuania, as well as other fellow EU members Poland, Slovakia and Hungary. Performance figures show that the country's **GDP** has grown by over 10% in recent years. In fact, post-independence economic growth has averaged around 6% per annum, with the government forecasting growth of 7–8% each year in the short-term future. This economic growth is comparable to that experienced by Latvia, but much faster than that of Lithuania.

A **stable economy**, which is pegged against the Euro, and the country's favourable tax system have also stimulated international trade relationships and encouraged significant levels of domestic and foreign investment.

THE PEOPLE
Population

According to the Department of Statistics of the Government of the Republic of Lithuania (Statistics Lithuania), **Lithuania's** population totalled almost **3.4 million** in 2007. This figure is 300,000 less than the pre-independence population of just over 3.7 million. This decline is partially attributable to both a falling birth rate (although this has begun to rise in recent years) and the repatriation of some Russian residents to their mother country.

Lithuania has **more female than male citizens**, with their respective proportions standing at 53.5% and 46.5%. This doesn't mean that you'll find a higher percentage of young, eligible ladies in the country, but rather that the **mortality rates** mirror those around the globe with women tending to live longer than men. In 2006 the **average life expectancy** for Lithuanian women was 77 years, with the average male living until just 65.

The town-country split in Lithuania's population reveals

a propensity towards **urban living**, with almost 2.3 million people living in built-up areas and just over 1.1 million residing in the countryside.

Data published by the country's Central Bureau of Statistics (CBS) showed that the **Latvian population** was almost **2.3 million** in 2007, although recent years have witnessed a small but steady decrease. A number of things contribute to the year-on-year decline in the Latvian population since 2004, including a falling birth rate, the continued decrease in the number of Russian citizens living in the country and the new freedom of movement that accompanied the country's EU accession.

Like Lithuania, Latvia's population has a **female** bias, with 54% (approximately 1,240,000) of the country's inhabitants women and 46% men (around 1,060,000). Again this is mainly due to the fact that women tend to live longer than men. In fact, over 70% of people aged 70 years or more are women, as are over 60% of people in the 65–69-year age group.

In common with industrial societies around the globe, the majority of Latvians have plumped for **urban living**. Over 30% of the population (723,000) live in the city of Rīga alone. Latvia's other **most populous cities** include Daugavpils (108,000), Liepāja (86,000), Jelgava (66,000), Jūrmala (55,000), Ventspils (44,000) and Rēzekne (36,000).

Data published by Statistics Estonia show that, in common with its Baltic siblings, the country's population has been experiencing a gradual decline since the beginning of the new millennium. In 2007 the population stood at just over **1,340,000**, compared to more than 1,360,00 in 2002. Again this decline will be partially attributable to emigration. Interestingly, the birth rate in **Estonia** has been increasing annually since 2004, and this trend might bring about future population growth.

In keeping with the populations of Lithuania and Latvia, approximately 54% of Estonian citizens are women and 46% men. Again this is due primarily to longer female life expectancy. The ratio of men to women in the 65–74-year age group is roughly 3:2, amongst 80–84-year-olds this ratio is 3:1, rising to 4:1 in the over 85s.

Above: *Estonian woman in traditional dress.*

The Livs are an ancient people who once ruled over swathes of the Baltic region, but now only cling on to a small section of the Latvian coast. After years of being ignored at best, real attempts are being made to record and preserve their unique language and culture. To delve more into the world of this tiny minority visit the cultural centre in Mazirbe and the sprinkling of Liv villages that hide amongst the wind ravaged Baltic dunes nearby.

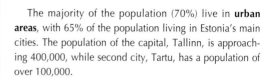

As a rule of thumb hand-shakes are often exchanged when meeting someone for the first time. If you are travelling on business then you should also exchange business cards with your Baltic counterpart. Although Lithuanians, Latvians and Estonians can all be fairly direct, they are not deliberately offensive and you should be careful not to cause offence either. Any attempts at speaking the local language will be greatly appreciated.

The majority of the population (70%) live in **urban areas**, with 65% of the population living in Estonia's main cities. The population of the capital, Tallinn, is approaching 400,000, while second city, Tartu, has a population of over 100,000.

Ethnic and Religious Mix

According to Statistics Lithuania approximately 85% of people living in Lithuania are **ethnic Lithuanians**. The next biggest ethnic group are **Poles**, who comprise about 6% of the population. Lithuania's other significant minority groups are **Russians** (5% of the population) and **Belarussians** (just 1% of the total population). Prior to 1991 the country's ethnic mix was roughly 80% Lithuanian, 10% Russian, 7% Polish and 2% Belarussian.

In a staunchly Catholic country where an overwhelming majority of the population are Lithuanian, it is perhaps no surprise that approximately 80% of the country's inhabitants are **Roman Catholic**. Roughly 4% of the population adhere to Russian Orthodox beliefs, while 2% belong to other Christian faiths

According to the CBS about 60% of people living in Latvia are **ethnic Latvians**. The next biggest ethnic group living in the country are **Russians**, who comprise around 28% of the population. A significant minority of Belarussians (85,000 people), Poles (55,000 people) and Lithuanians (31,000 people) also live in Latvia. The country is also home to a small number of Jews (10,000 people), Romas (8500 people), Germans (4200 people) and Estonians (2500 people).

With a majority Latvian population the two main religions are **Lutheran** and **Roman Catholic**. With such a sizeable Russian and Belarussian population, a significant number of people adhere to the **Russian Orthodox** faith. Small numbers of the population also follow other Christian faiths, as well as Judaism, Islam and Buddhism.

The majority of Estonia's inhabitants (around 70%) are **ethnic Estonians**. Around 25% of the population are **Russian**. The next biggest ethnic minorities are Ukrainian (roughly 2%) and Belarussian (approximately 1%). A small number of Finns, Tartars, Latvians, Poles, Jews, Lithuanians and Germans also live in Estonia.

Mirroring the country's ethnic make-up the majority religion in Estonia is **Lutheran**, closely followed by **Russian Orthodox**. Other Christian faiths and the Muslim faith also have followers in Estonia.

Opposite: *Religion plays a big part in life in all three Baltic States; here the devout attend a service in Rēzekne in Latvia.*

National Identity

Centuries of subjugation by other countries, a comparatively young democracy, a predominately Lithuanian population and hundreds of years spent cultivating a national consciousness has given **Lithuanians** a **strong national identity**. This is perhaps why Lithuanians, like their Baltic brothers and sisters, were secure enough within themselves to be willing to join the European Union in 2004, just 13 years after the country became independent.

Viewed from a different perspective, the country's embrace of European citizenship is the single biggest expression of a Lithuanian identity, which has long been **pro-European**. In everyday life a sense of what it means to be Lithuanian is kept alive by a shared language and culture, as well as the preservation of folk traditions. Food, drink and sporting achievement are also central to the Lithuanian sense of self.

With such a large proportion of ethnic Russian residents (over a quarter of the population) **Latvia** has what can best be described as a **complex national identity**. After the tough years of Soviet times, when ethnic Russian immigrants were often given the best jobs, some ethnic Latvians have a strong sense of patriotism. At the other end of the scale some Russians feel disenfranchised in the only country in which they have spent most or all of their lives. As the fledgling nation matures a more cohesive and inclusive sense of national identity may develop, though tensions over this thorny issue remain.

Inhabited by native Setus (considered to be the oldest settled people in Europe), Estonia's southeastern corner is known as Setumaa. It is estimated that around 1200 Setus live in Estonia and another 600 in Russia. The distinctive Setu culture has its own national costume, its own singing style (*leelo*) and dialect. Setus follow a mix of Estonian and Russian cultures; for example, although most Estonian Setus don't speak Russian they adhere to the Orthodox faith and built an Orthodox church in Obinitsa in 1952.

The struggle to free Estonia, Latvia and Lithuania from Soviet rule in the late 1980s and early 1990s has now become rather romantically known as the 'Singing Revolution'. The term was coined by Estonian artist Heinz Valk to describe the flowering movement of mass song festivals and singing demonstrations that swept the region between 1987 and 1991 in a re-awakening of nationalism that became an integral part of the road towards independence, with Estonia at the forefront.

Although a quarter of **Estonia's** population are **ethnic Russian** the country does have a keenly honed sense of national identity that sees the Estonians place themselves as a sort of bridge between Scandinavia and the Baltics. This is more than a simple geographical fact, but also comes across in their efficient attitude to business, the sleekness of Tallinn's new business buildings and the country's 'can do' approach. This carefully constructed national identity was dented in 2007 with the riots that followed the relocation of a Russian war memorial (see panel, page 96).

Culture and Folk Traditions

During Soviet times the local popular culture was tolerated at best, but **high culture** was invested in and opera and classical music are still of a high standard in the cities, especially Vilnius, today. Song is probably the single most important of Lithuania's traditions. Through the centuries *dainas* (folk songs) have played a pivotal role in events as diverse as weddings and war – to date over 500,000 folk songs have been recorded. Folk music is also a vehicle for passing down historical tales or mythical stories.

Song, in the form of the **Singing Revolution**, was also paramount to Lithuanian independence (see panel, this page). Staged across the country, **Song Festivals** continue to champion Lithuanian identity and preserve the past. Wooden trumpets (*daudytė*) and North Eastern panpipes (*skudučiai*) are amongst the traditional instruments accompanying the songs. Famous Lithuanian literary figures have included Kristijonas Donelaitis, author of the first epic poem in Lithuanian, renowned poet Adam Mickiewicz (whom the Lithuanians lay claim to) and Nobel Prize-winning poet and novelist Czesław Miłosz.

Since the awakening of the **Latvian national consciousness** (in the mid-19th century), paintings and songs have held an important place in the heart of Latvians everywhere. Champions of yesteryear include Krišjānis Barons (1835–1923) who penned and published the 'Latvju Dainas' collection of Latvian **folk songs**.

Andrejs Pumpurs (1841–1901), the author and poet who wrote the national epic *Lāčplēsis*, is another Latvian

Below: *Women dressed in traditional clothing for a folk festival in Latvia – festivals are crucial to preserving a sense of culture and identity in the Baltic States.*

folk hero. As you travel around the country, the names Jānis Rainis (1865–1929) and Rūdolfs Blaumanis (1863–1908) are also likely to crop up at regular intervals. The former, a playwright, poet and politician, is widely regarded as the best writer to come out of Latvia. The latter was another highly influential author and playwright.

In the arena of **art**, Jānis Rozentāls (1866–1917) is one of Latvia's most enduringly popular painters. The work of another renowned Latvian artist, Marko Rothko, is popular amongst Latvians, who see his paintings as an expression of the country's desire for freedom.

In common with the other Baltic States, Estonia has a strong **folk culture** that runs parallel to and complements its interest in classical performances; the majority of the latter are staged in Tallinn and Tartu. The 'National Awakening' in the 19th century brought F R Kreutzwald's (*see* page 120) efforts to preserve the rich folk culture and Lydia Koidula's native language poems and plays to the fore. More recently, Jann Kross's Nobel Prize-nominated novels have catered to a taste for a growing post-independence desire to discover the heritage of the nation through literature.

Above: *Cēsu beer, one of the most popular brands in beer-loving Latvia.*

Food and Drink

Like all the Baltic nations the **Lithuanian diet** features a large amount of red meat, often served up in hearty stews and broths to help people through the long, cold winter months. A very popular soup is *šaltibarščiai*, a warming beetroot-based soup, while Russian-style borsch also features on many menus. The local version of ravioli, *koldūnai*, is a tasty treat and is usually boiled, while *cepelinai*, or 'Zeppelin', a potato dumpling, is as close as the country gets to a national dish. In autumn mushroom dishes are a highlight, with legions of locals out picking them. Beer (*alus*) is ubiquitous with perhaps the best the hoppy Kalnapilis.

With its roots in rural peasant culture, **Latvian food** can best be described as 'hearty'. Red meat in various cream sauces and stew permutations can be found on many

You are more likely to be bitten by a dog or scratched by a cat than you are to be mauled by a hulking bear in the Baltics. That said, the region does pack in mammals that make venturing off for a hike in the woods that little bit more interesting. Chief suspects are the aforementioned bear, but also look out for the old wolf, as well as wild boar: the latter have been known to charge hikers daft enough to get in their way.

menus. A welcome change from meat is the fresh fish that comes both from the country's large Baltic coast and from its freshwater rivers and lakes. *Pīrāhi* are a hearty snack consisting of pasties filled with meat or cheese. *Pīrāhi* can also be found floating in soups, with thick broths and borsch on many restaurant menus. Beer is very popular, the two best brewers being Aldaris and Cēsu.

In common with the other Baltic countries **hearty meat dishes**, with their roots in the country's peasant traditions, are the mainstay on many Estonian menus. Of the three Baltic States, **Estonia** is where you are likely to find more salads and the culinary influences of Scandinavia creeping in. With a large swathe of Baltic Sea, seafood is popular too, the highlights being herring and salmon. Vodka and local liqueur Vana Tallinn compete for popularity with beer, with the most renowned brewer of the latter being Saku.

Below: *Rīga boasts the most impressive Art Nouveau architecture in Europe, with some of the finest examples on Elizabetes.*

Architecture

The various wars that have ravaged through the region have destroyed much of **Lithuania's architectural heritage** and preservation was not a priority during Soviet times when the over-use of concrete was seen as the way forward. That said, **Vilnius** is home to the second largest Baroque quarter in Europe and also boasts architectural flourishes from other periods. Outside the capital look out for traditional **wooden houses** in the countryside and **Baroque** in Kaunas, as well as numerous **castles**, with Trakai the obvious highlight.

Latvia is dotted with **old timber houses**. Many of the buildings that you see would have originally had a thatched roof, though it is rare to see thatching on new homes today. The Open-air Ethnographic Museum (*see* page 68) on the outskirts of the capital boasts a collection of these buildings. The seaside resort of Jūrmala is also distinct, with its array of wooden homesteads. For many, though, Latvia's **architectural highlights** are Francesco Bartolomeo Rastrelli's Rundāle Palace and the rich architectural tapestry that makes up Rīga's UNESCO World Heritage Old Town and Art Nouveau district.

In Estonia, the **old quarters** of Tartu, Pärnu and (especially) Tallinn are home to some fascinating old buildings, covering both Baroque and Medieval architectural styles. Tallinn is currently undergoing something of a transformation with many Soviet-era buildings being cleared to make way for the gleaming new glass-and-steel constructions that are a symbol of a city and country on the move. In the countryside look out for old **wooden houses** and lovely old **windmills**, the finest of which you will find on the island of Saaremaa.

Language

Lithuanian is a branch of the **Indo-European** family of languages. It is a very tricky language to learn, but any attempts to speak it, even just pleasantries, are much appreciated by the locals. Many modern English words are creeping into Lithuanian and most young people can speak fluent English, although the further you get away from Vilnius the proportion of English speakers drops. Other languages spoken in the country include Polish, German and Russian, though the latter is on the wane.

Latvian is another branch of the **Indo-European** family of languages. Like Lithuanian it is a difficult language to learn, but again any attempts to speak it will be looked on kindly by the locals. Modern English words are now more prevalent in Latvian and many of the younger generation speak fluent English. The further you travel from Riga, however, the smaller the number of English speakers. Russian, Polish and Ukranian are some of the other languages spoken in the country.

Estonian, in contrast to the other two languages, is a branch of the **Finno-Ugric** family of languages. It is a very complicated language to learn with 14 noun cases, but locals will appreciate your efforts, even simple pleasantries. Many modern English words are mixed into Estonian and the majority of young people can speak English fluently. In common with Lithuanian and Latvian, as you get further away from the capital the proportion of English speakers drops. Finnish and Russian are also widely spoken. The region has a number of different dialects in use.

ADVENTURE SPORTS

The Baltics will never be New Zealand or Scotland, but they are not the adrenaline sport desert that some people presume. The flat plains and rolling hills are ideal for cycling, while the expansive forests and scenic coastlines are great for hiking with an increasing number of trails being marked out. Then there are canoeing and rafting on the rivers and lakes. Skiing is becoming increasingly popular, particularly with the young.

2
Vilnius

Perhaps the least known of the three Baltic State capitals, Vilnius has for decades reclined in the shadows. All that has started to change since 2004 when Lithuania followed its recently acquired NATO membership by joining the European Union and opening up its capital's charms to a whole new market of business people and tourists. Savvy travellers and pioneering members of the business community had already discovered Vilnius, but it is the EU ascension that has really kicked things off.

The city's **UNESCO World Heritage** listed old core is stunning, centred around a well-preserved and expansive Baroque **Old Town** that is fringed by the Vilnia and Neris rivers. A riot of church spires reach for the heavens; just how many churches Vilnius has can be appreciated by climbing up to the city's castle or visiting one of the parks that dot this green metropolis.

On the north bank of the **Neris** a new Vilnius is taking shape, a 21st-century collage of glass-and-steel skyscrapers geared towards the burgeoning business community, a world that offers a complete contrast to Vilnius and Lithuania before the break from the Soviet Union and the ditching of communism in 1991.

Add in the buzz that the large local **student population** injects into the old streets and Vilnius today is a thrilling, energetic and rewarding place to visit whether on business or pleasure. Vilnius is still far less crowded than either Tallinn or Riga, but that has started to change following the massive attention the city gained as a 'European City of Culture' in 2009.

DON'T MISS

*** Cathedral Square: Vilnius's spiritual heart is an impressive set piece.
*** Lower and Higher Castle Museums: explore the remains of the city's old fortifications.
*** Church of St Peter and St Paul: one of the capital's most ornate churches.
** Gates of Dawn: 16th-century portal with deep religious significance.
** St Anne's Church: red-brick Gothic masterpiece.
** Lithuanian National Museum: providing a fascinating insight into Lithuania and its people.

Opposite: *The Lithuanian Presidential Palace is a striking building in Vilnius.*

EXPLORING VILNIUS

In effect the key sight is the **Old Town** itself, the largest
Baroque quarter in Europe outside Prague, with mile upon
mile of cobbled streets that are flanked by a riot of (increasingly) revamped Baroque beauties. Attractions include a
flurry of churches, the highlight of which is the striking
Cathedral, which lies below Vilnius Castle, itself a good
place to take in views of the city and get orientated.

Aušros Vartai **

The rather poetically named old city **Aušros vartai** (Gates
of Dawn) is one of the symbols of Vilnius and a deeply
devout spot for Catholics; many locals cross themselves
every time they pass under the arch. Dating as far back as
the 16th century, the old defensive structure is now home
to a delicate image of the Virgin Mary.

Katdros Aikste ***

The dramatic public expanse of **Katdros aikšte** (Cathedral
Square), on the site of an old pagan temple, lies at the physical and spiritual heart of the Lithuanian capital. It is home to
the starched white **Arkikatedra bazilika** (Vilnius Cathedral),
whose façade gleams brilliantly on a clear sunny day.

Look out for the trio of statues that crown the grand
columns: St Helena with the cross, Casimir (the patron saint
of Lithuania) and Stanisław, the Polish patron saint. Delve
past the school groups and head inside to admire the highlights of the Chapel of St Casimir, and the crypt, the latter only
accessible on guided tours, which allow you a peek at the
remains of a collection of Lithuanian and Polish nobles. Open
10:00–17:00 Monday–Saturday, 14:00–17:00 Sunday.

Standing guard right outside the cathedral's main door is
the **Arkikatedros varpinė** (Cathedral Clock Tower). This
hulking Baroque tower reaches improbably off into the
heavens and with the cathedral in the background forms
the city's most photographed scene.

Žemutinės Pilies Muziejus ir
Aukštutinės Pilies Muziejus ***

Directly behind the cathedral are the rambling remains of

the **Žemutinės pilies muziejus** (Lower Castle Museum). In the 16th century the Grand Duke of Lithuania (and also King of Poland) held court here on a grand scale with a library alone that contained thousands of books, though little of the original survived Tsarist rule. The go-getting new millennium Lithuanian politicians are extremely keen on rebuilding something as close to the original as possible, though how successful the end result is remains to be seen. Open by appointment.

Rambling uphill from the Lower Museum is the aptly named **Aukštutinės pilies muziejus** (Higher Castle Museum), home to what remains of Vilnius Castle. The sturdy red-brick Gediminas Tower on top offers great views of the city and you have the option of walking up or taking the new funicular. The tower's museum illuminates how the castle took shape over the centuries. Open daily 10:00–19:00.

Above: *Vilnius Cathedral and its hulking clock tower are two of the most popular attractions in the Lithuanian capital.*

Šv. Onos Bažnyčia ★★

A fine example of late Gothic, **Šv. Onos bažnyčia** (St Anne's Church) is a highlight in a city overflowing with remarkable houses of prayer. Napoleon Bonaparte is said to have been a fan; so much so that the ambitious emperor was said to have even considered shifting the whole construction back to Paris.

Šv. Petro ir Povilo Bažnyčia ★★★

The epic **Šv. Petro ir Povilo bažnyčia** (Church of St Peter and St Paul), a short walk east along the river, is breathtaking. Remodelled to celebrate the city's escape from a ten-year Russian siege in the 17th century, the interior of the church is a riot of stuccowork. If you stare all day you will keep discovering something new – in total, Italian craftsmen Pietro Perti and Giovanni Maria Galli spent over a decade stuffing every available space with their ornate icons, figures and overflowing stucco fruit.

CHURCHES

You could spend a week or two mining Vilnius's rich seam of churches and no visit to the city is complete without a

JEWISH VILNIUS

Vilnius boasted a thriving Jewish community in the approach to World War II. The Nazis, with some local collaboration, set about destroying it with many of the victims murdered out at Paneriai. In town you can trace out two of the old Jewish districts and note the brace of Yiddish signs on Žemaitijos, the small Holocaust Museum and a sprinkling of Jewish cultural centres, where you can learn Yiddish and buy Vilnius's Jewish newspaper.

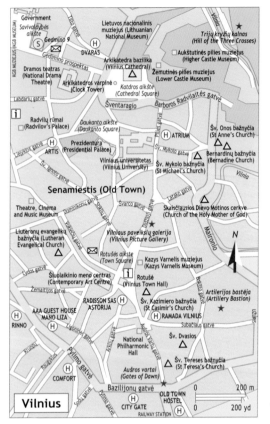

visit to at least two or three. Often the best plan is to pick a few you like the sound of then choose one 'wild card' that will be a complete surprise. Those listed below are amongst the most interesting:

Bernardinų Bažnyčia

The **Bernardinų bažnyčia** (Bernadine Church) is notable for its Baroque exterior and the frescoes that lie inside.

Šv. Mykolo Bažnyčia

Šv. Mykolo bažnyčia (St Michael's Church) lost its ecclesiastical role in 1948 during a Soviet clampdown and today it houses the local Architecture Museum.

Šv. Kazimiero Bažnyčia

Napoleon did not rate the Jesuits' 17th-century **Šv. Kazimiero bažnyčia** (St Casimir's Church), and his armies put it to use as a grain store. The church's rich history is every bit as interesting as its architecture.

Šv. Tereses Bažnyčia

The Baroque exterior and the interior frescoes are the highlights at **Šv. Tereses bažnyčia** (St Teresa's Church).

Skaisčiausios Dievo Motinos Cerkve

A very different style is adopted by the **Skaisčiausios Dievo Motinos cerkve** (Church of the Holy Mother of God), the city's largest Orthodox place of worship.

MUSEUMS
Lietuvos Nacionalinis Muziejus ★★

Housed in one of the city's old arsenal buildings the **Lietuvos nacionalinis muziejus** (Lithuanian National Museum) is a cultural highlight, which sheds light on both the capital and the country. Common to the region, much attention is given over to images of how people used to live when the country was predominantly rural. Other intriguing artefacts include an old executioner's sword and an Egyptian sarcophagus. The upper level focuses more on Vilnius itself with historic weapons, currency and cutlery all on show. Look out too for the separate part of the museum given over to Lithuania's prehistoric heritage, which covers some of the earliest of the Baltic settlers. Open 10:00–17:00 Tue–Sat, 10:00–15:00 Sun, closed Mon (summer); 10:00–18:00 Wed–Sun, closed Mon and Tue (winter).

KGB Muziejus ★

The dark days of Soviet occupation come alive at the chilling **KGB muziejus** (KGB Museum). The exhibits are housed in the actual building where anyone who had rankled the authorities was held, tortured and then often either executed or condemned to the gulags. The cells in the basement, which were used right up to independence in 1991, are particularly chilling, as is the old execution chamber. Open daily 10:00–17:00.

AROUND TOWN
Gedimino ★

The grand **Gedimino** boulevard was looking fairly shabby on independence in 1991 and then it endured a decade being taken over by the city's increasing traffic. These days it has been seriously tarted up with wider pedestrian-friendly pavements and many of its ornate façades have been brought back to their best. Here you will find globally famous retail names nestling alongside the home-grown outfits and the sprinkling of bars, cafés and restaurants.

Prezidentura ★

The neoclassical grandeur of the **Prezidentura** (Presidential

---

FRANK ZAPPA

Rather confusingly legendary rock oddball Frank Zappa has absolutely no connection with Vilnius or indeed Lithuania, but a statue of him now stands in the capital. This is perhaps more due to the pioneering attitudes of the newly independent nation in the 1990s, when the local authorities were reluctant to say no to anything, rather than a national love for Zappa.

NIGHTLIFE

When independence came in 1991 Vilnius nightlife was not exactly lively, unless of course you were a senior member of 'The Party' or enjoyed smoky dives with dubious quality beer. These days Vilnius's nightlife buzzes with the Old Town awash with nocturnal haunts, with everything from old-world pubs right through to trendy bars. The action also spills out on to Gedimino. Both areas sport pavement tables in summer, while revellers retreat indoors during the colder months.

USEFUL LITHUANIAN PHRASES

Laba diena • hello/good day
Viso gero • goodbye
Parašu, parašom • please
Ačiū • thank you
Kiek kainuoja? • how much?
Ligoninė • hospital
Aerouostas • airport
Vienas, viena • one
Dvi, du • two
Trys • three
Keturi, keturios • four
Penki, penkios • five
Šeši, Šešios • six
Septyni, septynios • seven
Aštuoni, aštuonios • eight
Devyni, devynios • nine
Dešimt • 10
Šimtas • 100

Palace) is hard to miss and is an Old Town highlight. Sitting at the head of a sparse square it rears up with its neat columns and fluttering Lithuanian tricolour flags. The actual building has enjoyed a chequered history, home to various figures down the years such as the Bishop of Vilnius and Tsarist officials. Local legend has it that poet Adam Mickiewicz was once imprisoned and interrogated within the walls where the Lithuanian president now resides.

Užupis

The wacky side of Vilnius bubbles just below the surface most of the time, but in the **Užupis** district, which rambles up a hillside east of the Old Town, it positively bubbles over. This 'independent republic' (declared on April Fool's Day in 2000) is a ramshackle affair with a motley collection of houses that are inhabited by a bohemian collage of artists and writers, but also increasingly by young professionals priced out of the Old Town. Užupis is nothing if not eclectic and there always seems to be something on, though it is unlikely the city tourist office will be able to fill you in. Instead head for Užupio, a bar at the heart of the local scene where the staff can let you know about any local 'happenings' during your visit.

Vilniaus Universitetas

Right in the heart of the Old Town is the lovely old **Vilniaus universitetas** (Vilnius University). You can explore much of the campus on foot, flitting between the various courtyards and taking in the eclectic sweep of architecture, which covers various styles from the 16th century right through to the modern day. To actually get inside the university buildings you will need to be on a guided tour. Highlights include **St John's Church**, with its elegant façade, and the **Smugliewicz Hall**, with its impressive frescoes. Open Mon–Sat 10:00–18:00, closed Sun (summer); Mon–Sat 10:00–17:00, closed Sun (winter).

PANERIAI

Out in the lush forests on the fringes of the city lurks a site draped in Nazi evil. Amongst the trees and the old Russian oil storage pits an estimated 100,000 people, including a large swathe of Vilnius's Jewish population, were butchered by German troops. Today a simple communist-era memorial marks the site and there is also a museum that details the hideous crimes committed here.

Trijų Kryžių Kalnas

The trio of crosses, which were originally placed on the **Trijų kryžių kalnas** (Hill of the Three Crosses) during the

17th century, marked the crucifixion of a group of monks. In World War I three stone crosses were built to celebrate the withdrawal of the Russians, and quickly became both symbolic of faith and the Lithuanian national identity. Unsurprisingly, the Soviets were not too pleased and they were destroyed by Stalin's regime in 1950. Again they rose, this time when they were rebuilt as the country approached independence. The views of the city are excellent from up here and the walks back down the wooded slopes are part of the fun.

OUTSIDE THE CITY CENTRE
Televizijos Bokštas
The **Televizijos bokštas** (Television Tower) boasts the most comprehensive panorama of the city, but is not ideal for vertigo sufferers. There is a small café but it is the 360° views that people take the lift up to savour. Look out also for the touching exhibition commemorating the sacrifice of 14 civilians who were murdered by Soviet tanks in 1991 during the independence struggle. Their sacrifice is remembered today both by a simple exhibition showcasing the tragic events of those tumultuous days and also by a clutch of wooden crosses by the tower. Open daily 10:00–22:00.

Europos Parkas (Europe Park)
This large sculpture park is located at the supposed exact centre of Europe, 10km (6 miles) out of Vilnius, though the French National Geographic Institute who originally 'located' it in 1989 have now come out and said the real centre may actually lie a few kilometres away; perhaps it is best not to mention this to the park staff before they let you in. **Europos parkas** (Europe Park), which stretches across 55ha (136 acres), was founded in 1991 by Lithuanian sculptor Gintaras Karosas. It functions as an open-air museum showcasing the country's art, but is equally enjoyable as a green space for strolling around on a sunny day. The rolling hills and woodland are sprinkled with sculptures and art installations. Guided tours are the best way to get the most out of the park and are available in English.

Below: *Vilnius Television Tower swirls in tales of tragedy and today the memorials there to the citizens who were killed in the struggle for independence in 1991 are a sobering reminder to tourists ascending the tower for a view.*

Vilnius at a Glance

Sunny spring and summer days make **May–September** the best time to visit Vilnius. During this main tourist season bars and cafés bring their tables out into the streets. In spring and early autumn it can still be cold at night, so pack a jumper or coat. Winters are cold (rarely rising above 0°C/32°F between December and March) but drier.

Rail: Domestic routes run to Vilnius from Kaunas, Klaipėda, Trakai and Šiauliai.
Road: Numerous Lithuanian towns, including Druskininkai, Kaunas, Palanga, Trakai and Klaipėda, have direct **bus services** to the capital.

The old core of Vilnius is easy to explore on **foot**, with **buses**, **trolleybuses** and **taxis** on hand to get to out-of-town sights.

LUXURY
Ramada Vilnius, Subačiaus 2, tel: (5) 255 3355, fax: (5) 255 3311, www.ramada vilnius.lt Enjoying a central location and offering all the trimmings that you'd expect to find in a four-star hotel, as well as free use of the Jacuzzi/sauna room, the Ramada is a real winner.

Radisson SAS Astorija, Didžioji 35/2, tel: (5) 212 0110, fax: (5) 212 1762, www.radissonsas.com Also situated at the heart of the Old Town, this plush and elegant hotel, which successfully marries Lithuanian Baroque and the five-star service that the Scandinavian hotel chain is renowned for, is a strong contender for Vilnius's best hotel.
Holiday Inn, Seimyniskiu 1, tel: (5) 210 3000, fax: (05) 210 3001, www.holiday innvilnius.lt Located at the city's business heart on the north bank of the River Neris, the Holiday Inn has modern hi-tech rooms. If you can't bag an Old Town room then this is a good option.
Hotel Artis, Liejyklos 11/23, tel: (5) 266 0366, fax: (05) 266 0377, www.centrum hotels.com Housed in a handsome 19th-century building at the heart of the Old Town, the Artis currently has 65 bedrooms. By the end of 2008 there should be 120 rooms. Guests can also use a small pool and gym.

MID-RANGE
City Gate, Bazilijonų 3, tel: (5) 210 7306, fax: (5) 210 7307, www.citygate.lt A handy location close to the Gates of Dawn, good spec rooms and its small size (there are just 24 bedrooms) make this hotel a great option.

Panorama, Sodų 14, tel: (5) 233 8822, fax: (5) 233 5832, www.hotelpanorama.lt If you are hankering after a room with a view but don't want to break the bank, then check in here. The accommodation is comfortable with a surprising number of frills.
Rinno, Vingrių 25, tel: (5) 262 2828, fax: (5) 262 5929, www.rinno.lt This Scandinavian three-star at the heart of the Old Town has modern rooms, with large bathrooms and good views a bonus in some.
AAA Guest House 'Mano Liza', Ligoninės 5, tel: (5) 212 2225, fax: (5) 212 2608, www.hotelinvilnius.lt This cosy 8-room and apartment guesthouse boasts comfortable accommodation and enjoys a quiet Old Town location. Breakfast is included.

BUDGET
Jeruzale, Kalvarijų 247, tel: (5) 271 4040, fax: (5) 276 2627 www.jeruzalehotel.com Located 10 minutes' walk north of the River Neris the Jeruzale provides basic but comfortable accommodation at affordable prices. The small pool, sauna and in-room Internet access are a surprising bonus.
Victoria, Saltoniskiu 56, tel: (5) 272 4013, fax: (5) 272 4320, www.victoria.lt Offering clean and comfortable rooms just 10 minutes' walk from the Old Town.

Vilnius at a Glance

AAA Hostel, Šv. Stepeno 15, tel: 6801 8557, www.ahostel.lt Enjoying an Old Town location close to both the bus and railway stations, as well as rock bottom prices for a bed in 4- or 8-person dormitories, the bright and funky AAA Hostel is popular with backpackers.

Old Town Hostel, Aušros Vartų 20-15, tel: (5) 262 5357, fax: (5) 268 5967, www.lithuanianhostels.org With 25 beds in double, triple and quad rooms, as well as dormitories, this is a flexible central option. Free Internet access.

WHERE TO EAT

La Provence, Voliečių 22, tel: (5) 262 0257, www.laprovence.lt Chefs at this fine-dining restaurant conjure up mouth-watering dishes from across the Mediterranean. Slick service and attention to detail provide the finishing touches.

Pegasus, Didžioji 11, tel: (5) 260 9430, www.restaurant pegasus.lt The menu at this trendy restaurant is, some would say, a fusion of Italian, French and Indian dishes. The minimalist interior and friendly service make it popular with the local in-crowd.

Stikliai, Gaono 7, tel: (5) 264 9580. A refined ambience and equally fine food ensures the signature restaurant at the Stikliai Hotel a place amongst Lithuania's best restaurants; of course these things come at a price.

Tores, Užupio 40, tel: (5) 262 9309, www.tores.lt A personal favourite, this restaurant-cum-art gallery-cum-wine cellar. A real find in the artsy/grungy Užupis quarter, this bar-restaurant serves good and reasonably priced food boasts. Overlooking the River Vilnia and Upper Castle your meal also comes with a great view.

SHOPPING

A mishmash of souvenirs ranging from dolls wearing traditional costume and amber to an assortment of tacky knick-knacks are predominantly located in the **Old Town** streets of **Didžoji**, **Aušros Vartų** and **Pilies**. The latter is also home to the **Suvenyrų Turgų** (Souvenir Market). You can also pick up keepsakes from the **Tourist Information Centre**. International and local fashion stores, meanwhile, can be found near the Town Hall. For Lithuanian designer gear try **Stiklių**. **Gedimino prospekts** is also brimming with shopping opportunities. For local colour, literally, head to the **Gėlių Turgus**

Flower Market on **Basanavičiaus**. Also try Gariūinai market off the Kaunus Road. Open until lunch time, closed Mondays.

TOURS AND EXCURSIONS

A number of companies offer Vilnius city tours, both on **foot** and by **bus**. Regular **walking tours** run by **Vilnius City Tour** last two and a half hours. The company also organizes excursions further afield to destinations like **Trakai**, **Kaunas**, the **Pažaislis Monastery**, **Aukštaitija National Park** and the **Curonian Spit**.

USEFUL CONTACTS

Tourist Information Centre, Vilniaus 22, tel: (5) 262 9660, www.vilnius-tourism.lt **Railway Station**, Geležinkelio 16, tel: (5) 233 0088. **Bus Station**, Sodų 22, tel: 1661 (in Vilnius or from a mobile phone) or (5) 9000 1661, www.toks.lt **Vilnius City Tour**, tel: (5) 261 5558, www. vilniuscitytour.com

VILNIUS	J	F	M	A	M	J	J	A	S	O	N	D
AVERAGE TEMP. °C	-5	-4	-1	5	12	16	17	16	12	6	1	-3
AVERAGE TEMP. °F	23	24	30	41	53	60	62	60	53	42	33	26
RAINFALL mm	41	38	39	46	62	77	78	71	65	53	57	55
RAINFALL in	1.6	1.5	1.5	1.8	2.4	3.0	3.1	2.8	2.6	2.1	2.2	2.2
DAYS OF RAINFALL	19	14	13	13	12	14	16	13	16	15	18	22

3
Coastal Lithuania

Lithuania's coastline may be just 99km (62 miles) long, but what it lacks in size it more than makes up for with sights and scenic beauty. Indeed, some of Europe's most impressive coastal scenery is on display in the form of the epic sand dunes of the **Curonian Spit National Park**. This protected reserve is one of the Baltic States highlights, a strange netherworld, which can only be reached by ferry, of vaulting dunes that are spiced up by the Russian military installations shimmering across the haze in the distance.

The coast's city is **Klaipėda**, a bustling port that is slowly recovering from the loss of its Cold War markets with increasing trade with Western Europe and a burgeoning tourist industry. Then there is **Palanga**, a no-holds-barred party place that really comes alive in the summer months when it seems as if the whole country arrives to let their hair down.

Slipping down to the south of the coast just before the mainland border with Russia the highlight is the **Nemunas Delta Regional Park**, an impressive wetland environment with rich bird life that is best explored by boat. Sitting on a boat here on a sunny day watching the birds swoop around as you feast on fresh locally smoked fish and quaff an ice cold Lithuanian beer, you can congratulate yourself on taking the time to visit a small but deeply impressive coastline that all too recently was largely off limits to foreigners.

DON'T MISS

*** Curonian Spit National Park: a mystical landscape of towering sand dunes that is only accessible by ferry.
** Nida: this old fishing village-cum-low-key resort is the most charming settlement on the Curonian Spit.
** Klaipėda: a bustling port city.
* Nemunas Delta: a beautiful wetland now protected as a regional park.
* The Ventė Cape: a haven for bird life and boasts a pretty lighthouse.

KLAIPĖDA **

This busy port city lies in a sheltered location at the very northern end of the Curonian Lagoon on a narrow channel that separates the lagoon from the Baltic Sea. The third largest

Opposite: *Klaipėda Theatre Square boasts some impressive architecture.*

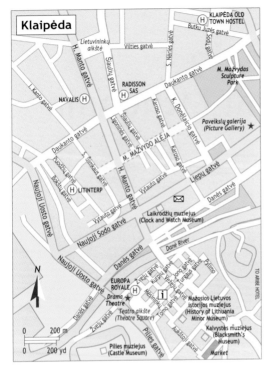

Klaipėda

KLAIPĖDA OLD TOWN HOSTEL (H)
Butkų Juzės gatvė
Sodų gatvė
S. Nėries gatvė
Lietuvininkų aikštė
Vilties gatvė
H. Manto gatvė
Šiaulių gatvė
Daukanto gatvė
M. Mozvydas Sculpture Park
RADISSON SAS (H)
I. Kanto gatvė
NAVALIS (H)
Karoso gatvė
K. Donelaičio gatvė
Paveikslų galerija (Picture Gallery) ★
Daukanto gatvė
Liegninės gatvė
Šiaulių gatvė
Puodžių gatvė
Bokštų gatvė
M. MAŽVYDO ALĖJA
S. Šimkaus gatvė
H. Manto gatvė
Karoso gatvė
Vytauto gatvė
Liepų gatvė
(H) LITINTERP
Danės gatvė
Naujoji Uosto gatvė
Vytauto gatvė
Laikrodžių muziejus (Clock and Watch Museum)
Naujoji Sodo gatvė
Danė River
Danės gatvė
Dané River
Naujoji Uosto gatvė
Naujoji Sodo gatvė
Žvejų gatvė
Žvejų gatvė
Kurpių gatvė
Jono gatvė
Turgaus gatvė
Pylimo
TO ARBE HOTEL
EUROPA ROYALE (H)
Mėsininkų gatvė
Tomo gatvė
Drama ★ Theatre
Teatro aikštė (Theatre Square)
i
Mažosios Lietuvos istorijos muziejus (History of Lithuania Minor Museum)
Žvejų gatvė
Pilies gatvė
Kalvystės muziejus (Blacksmith's Museum)
Aukštoji gatvė
Aukštoji gatvė
Pilies muziejus (Castle Museum)
Market

N

0   200 m
0   200 yd

city in the country, with a population of almost 200,000, **Klaipėda** is a city on the up and up as its port opens up to pan-Baltic trade and a new market in visiting cruise liners.

The go-getting local authorities have only recently realized the tourist potential of Klaipėda and have invested in the cruise ship facilities.

KLAIPĖDA OLD TOWN

The highlight of a visit to Klaipėda is its **Old Town**. It is perhaps unsurprising then that the city authorities have thrown money at its rejuvenation. This has brought the best out of its old Germanic merchant houses and cobbled streets. The Old Town is the legacy of the days when Klaipėda was the German city of Memel, a name it first acquired when Teutonic Knights set up shop in the region during the 13th century and which it retained until becoming part of Lithuania in 1923.

Teatro Aikšte

Teatro aikšte (Theatre Square) is the grandest square in Klaipėda, named after the suitably grand 19th-century theatre that dominates one flank. Two performances during its rich history stand out: that of the composer and conductor Wagner and that of Adolf Hitler. Hitler stood on the balcony here triumphantly bringing the city into the Third Reich in 1939.

Today the square is filled during the warmer months with souvenir stalls peddling amber and other keepsakes.

Look out for the fountain that is dedicated to the poet Simon Dach, depicting his heroine Ännchen von Tharau. This current incarnation only dates back to 1989 when it was rebuilt using photographs of the original, itself spirited off by the occupying Russians.

Mažosios Lietuvos Istorijos Muziejus

From its home in an impressive 18th-century building, the regional history museum, **Mažosios Lietuvos istorijos muziejus** (History of Lithuania Minor Museum), does its best to tell the story of Klaipėda and the surrounding region over the last ten millennia. Highlights in the 80,000-strong collection include a model of what the old city of Memel once looked like and another model of an old pagan site here. Then there are the usual exhibits of old currency, costumes, archaeological finds and the like. Look out too for a grainy photo marking Adolf Hitler's triumphant visit to the city. Open daily 10:00–18:00.

Other Museums

Klaipėda boasts a sprinkling of museums that are worth checking out if you have time. The **Kalvystės muziejus** (Blacksmith's Museum) is situated in an old blacksmith's workshop and you can still witness the skills of the craftsmen at work in a forge that unusually still functions today. Exhibits further showcase their skills with all sorts of wrought-iron creations on display. Open Tuesday–Saturday 10:00–18:00, closed Sunday and Monday.

The **Laikrodžių muziejus** (Clock and Watch Museum) boasts centuries of clock design, from old candle clocks right through to some rather chic 10th-century affairs. Open Tuesday–Sunday 10:00–17:00, closed Monday.

Klaipėdos Valstybinis Jūrų Uostas

The rambling **Klaipėdos valstybinis jūrų uostas** (Klaipėda State Seaport) was once the only ice-free Baltic port for the Soviet Union. As such it assumed massive strategic importance for Moscow, so much so that it was off limits to foreign nationals and access for Lithuanians was also controlled. These days numerous international companies

---

CLIMATE

Coastal Lithuania has a temperate climate, which means that summer days (June–August) and late spring/early autumn days (May and September) are pleasantly warm. In summer the average temperature hovers at around 16°C (61°F), but regularly exceeds 20°C (68°F) during the day. The city also benefits from 8–10 hours of sun each day between May and September. Winters are slightly warmer in coastal Lithuania than they are in the hinterland, with these only falling below 0°C (32°F) on a frequent basis in January and February.

AMBER FOLKLORE

The Lithuanians have a rather dreamy version of how amber came to be sprinkled along their coastline. Local folklore has it that Jūrate, the legendary Queen of the Baltic Sea, incurred the wrath of the Gods and they showed their displeasure by obliterating her lavish underwater palace complex. The amber that is still found today is said to be fragments of the hallowed palace.

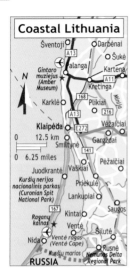

Coastal Lithuania

Šventoji
Darbėnai
Šukė
A13
Gintaro
muziejus
(Amber
Museum)
Palanga
Kartena
A11
Kretinga
168
Plikiai
Minija
A13
216
Klaipėda
E272
Vėžaičiai
0   12.5 km
Smiltynė
Gargždai
141
0   6.25 miles
Pėžaičiai
Juodkrantė
Vaškiai
Kuršių nerijos
nacionalinis parkas
(Curonian Spit
National Park)
167
Priekulė
Lankupiai
Saugos
Ragany
kalnas
Kintai
Ventė
Šilutė
Nida
Ventė ragas
(Ventė Cape)
Rusnė
Kuršių marios
Nemuno Delta
Regional Park
RUSSIA

pass goods through the increasingly busy port, which is a cornerstone of the local economy. The best way to get a real feel for the port is to go on a boat tour of the facilities. You will soon appreciate the mammoth scale as you creep around below hulking cranes and massive ships that are registered in all parts of the globe.

Kuršių Nerijos Nacionalinis Parkas ***

This spectacular natural escape of the **Kuršių nerijos nacionalinis parkas** (Curonian Spit National Park) will both metaphorically and often literally take your breath away, as it is a lonely, unspoiled landscape wide open to the ravages of the wild Baltic Sea. In few other places in the world can you enjoy such epic scenery, but still find your idyllic stroll along the sands interrupted by watchtowers and machine gun-toting sentries who don't seem to have been informed that the Cold War is over.

The only way on to the Curonian Spit, which is also known as the Neringa Spit, is by boat, with regular passenger and car ferries running from Klaipėda. The spit itself is 97km (60 miles) long, but only the northern half is part of Lithuania, with the south very much still part of the Russian geopolitical anomaly of Kaliningrad, a part of Russia despite the fact that since 1991 it shares no land border with the new Russian Federation.

A sinuous strip of land that is never more than 4km (2.5 miles) wide, and often much narrower in places, eases south with the Baltic to the west and the Curonian Lagoon to the east. The whole spit is basically one big undulating, partly submerged sand dune that shifts with the winds and the tides. Most striking are the large, barren dunes that look as if they have been shipped in from Arabia, while much of the sand is covered in a coating of pine trees and other low-lying vegetation. Wildlife to look out for includes everything from foxes, badgers and squirrels through to deer, wild boar and even elk.

Although the whole spit is protected as part of the Curonian Spit National Park only some of the more fragile dunes are off limits to the pub-

Below: *The Curonian Spit National Park is home to some of Europe's most impressive sand dunes, hulking towers of sand that rise like skyscrapers from the Baltic Sea.*

lic. Elsewhere you can often roam freely amongst the dunes, forests and beaches. There are even some villages dotted amongst the dunes as well as restaurants, bars and cafés servicing the needs of both tourists and Klaipėda weekend breakers.

SMILTYNĖ
The most northerly settlement on the Curonian Spit is home to an **Ethnographic Museum**. The exhibits are divided into two main sections, one looking at traditional wooden house building and the other, much more interesting, display focusing on all sorts of craft that once plied the testing locals waters of both the lagoon and the Baltic.

NIDA ***
Around Nida
Nida is perhaps the most charming settlement on the Curonian Spit. Having first grown as a fishing village, these days it is more given over to the needs of tourism with a sprinkling of restaurants and cafés lining the waterfront. The architectural highlight are the old **wooden houses** that were built either for the local people to live in or for holidaying Germans who first came here in the 19th century.

As people still live in many of these pretty little houses it is unlikely that you will see inside one, unless you visit the homestead on Nagliu that is now open as a **museum**. Here in this wonderfully unpretentious place you can delve back through the years imagining life as a local fisherman. If you think it is quite cramped then spare a though for the original inhabitants, as it would once have held not one but two families. To see where many of them are buried check out the fascinating cemetery that sprawls over the hillside by the **parish church** at the far end of Pamario. For the best view of Nida's lovely locale and of the impressive **Parnidis** dune head up to the solar clock on the hillside south of Nida. The clock was damaged during fierce storms, but the view remains.

Kuršių Nerijos Ekspozicija
Housed in a modern building this comprehensive museum has some fine examples of the local *kurenas* and *kiudelvatis*,

Above: *The house where Thomas Mann sought inspiration in Nida is well preserved today as a testament to the great writer and his love of the Curonian Spit village.*

both types of traditional boat. The **Kuršių nerijos ekspozicija** (Curonian Spit Exhibition) tracks the development of Nida from as far back as Neolithic times right through to when it first grew as a tourist resort and on to the present day. Visitors of a nervous disposition might want to avoid the section detailing the days when Nida residents had a penchant for eating crows and would catch them in nets before finishing them off with a bite to the neck. Open Tuesday–Sunday 11:00–19:00 May–September; closed October–April.

Tomo Manno Namelis

You can see why Thomas Mann was inspired to write at this cute little Nida house. The German author spent three summers here in the 1930s and penned large tracts of both *Young Joseph* and *The Story of Jacob* here. As well as editions of these titles, other exhibits in the modest collection at the **Tomo Manno namelis** (Thomas Mann House) include a photo of the author's enthusiastic welcome in Nida in 1930. Mann described the local scenery as resembling the balmy Mediterranean with its sands and blue skies; obviously he never visited in winter. Open Tuesday–Sunday 11:00–17:00 May–September; closed October–April.

Raganų Kalnas

Local legend has it that since time immemorial the Festival of St John was celebrated at the **Raganų kalnas** (Hill of the Witches) to the north of Nida near the village of Juodkrantė. Today the spooky hillside is laden with vaulting pine trees and 71 outdoor sculptures. These were sculpted out of oak tree during summers of 1979–81 by Lithuanian folk artists.

WALK THE LINE

Keen hikers can get over their frustration at the Baltics' lack of mountains by embarking on a spectacular trail along the Lithuanian coastline. The track on the Curonian Spit runs all the way south from Juodkrantė right down to the brink of the border with the Russian enclave of Kaliningrad. It can be done in summer as one very long, tough day, but most people choose to spread it over a few days, using local accommodation and even the minibuses that stop at the four car parks en route.

Thematically the focus is on witches, demons and local legends, making this an intriguing but scary place for younger travellers to Neringa. In 1988 another 12 sculptures were added, perhaps in an attempt to brighten things up a bit, with additions like swings and seats. The process of adding more sculptures continues; ask locally for a printed guide to what each one is meant to depict and allow at least a couple of hours for exploring the steep hillside.

ELSEWHERE ON THE COAST
Palanga

When you arrive in the Baltic beach resort of **Palanga** you should leave your pretensions firmly behind, especially if it is during the summer. Just north of Klaipėda the main strip of Basanavičiaus feels more like a suburb of Klaipėda or Vilnius when the mercury shoots up and people flock for fun in the Baltic sun. Palanga has always held a special place in the hearts and minds of Lithuanians as they have always seen it as 'theirs' while the Germanic visitors flocked to the Curonian Spit.

Yes, there are better beach resorts in many other places in Europe, but for just kicking back for a few days Palanga works. Don't forget to take a walk to the end of the wooden pier that juts out from the middle of the resort, a favourite of Lithuanian tourists. There are also a few traces of Palanga's history as a small fishing village and some interesting wooden architecture to keep more cerebral types engaged.

Other attractions include the **Botanical Gardens**, which date back to the 19th century (open Tuesday–Sunday 10:00–18:30, closed Monday), and the **Gintaro muziejus** (Amber Museum) that covers both amber in its pure form and the jewellery that is conjured up from it (open Tuesday–Sunday 10:00–18:00, closed Monday). A worthwhile winter garden lies within striking distance at Kretinga. A more sombre site is the simple granite **Žydų Genocido vieta** (Genocide Memorial), which marks the dark days of 1941 when the local Jewish population was spirited off to the concentration camps, many never to be seen alive again.

Above: *The Ventė ragas ranger station, where birds massively outnumber humans, feels on the edge of both Lithuania and the world.*

Nemuno Delta *

The aquatic wonderland of the **Nemuno delta** (Nemunas Delta) is often overlooked by those making a beeline for the Curonian Spit, but it is well worth the trip right to the south of the country's coastline. Protected as a national park since the early 1990s, much of it is pretty inaccessible to man anyway, given that the majority is made up of waterways, clogged-up channels and sparse islands. The local tourist people have got a little bit too excited in dubbing Nemanus the 'Lithuanian Venice' but it is fun to explore on a boat trip. These ease out around the wetlands and can include drinks and a chance to savour the delicious locally smoked fresh fish.

The largest settlement in the delta is Rusnė, with an information office where you can book boat tours, and in summer they also run ferries across to Nida on the Curonian Spit, saving you a lot of public transport hassles if you don't have your own wheels. Rusnė is said to be the lowest place in Lithuania.

Ventė Ragas *

For a real end-of-the-world experience head to **Ventė ragas** (the Ventė Cape), a wild, windswept outpost on the very edge of the delta (and the world). There is not that much to see here apart from a photogenic lighthouse, with a colony of birds often sitting handily as a backdrop, and an **Ornithological Museum**. They are said to have tagged hundreds of thousands of birds here and observed over 200 species, making this something of an ornithologist's paradise. Tours here are quite 'old school' with wonderfully eccentric guides producing live birds at various points and most of the exhibits being a wide collection of stuffed avians. Just being here in this remote spot is the main reason to visit.

Coastal Lithuania at a Glance

For a dip in the sea, the warm summer months are the best time to visit. **Spring** and **autumn** are also good times to visit, with quiet beaches great for an invigorating stroll.

Rail: Daily trains run to Klaipėda from Plungė, Kaunas and Vilnius. **Road:** Buses from Kaunas and Vilnius run to Klaipėda, Nida and Palanga.

Buses connect Klaipėda, Plungė and Palanga, as well as Nida, Klaipėda and Palanga. The best way to explore most places is on **foot**, although larger settlements have local **bus** services. To really explore the coast you will need a **car**.

LUXURY
Europa Royale, Žvejų 21/Teatro 1, Klaipėda, tel: (46) 404 444, www.group europa.com Central 50-room, four-star hotel.
Hotel Navalis, H. Manto 23, Klaipėda, tel: (46) 404 200, http://navalis.lt Centrally located hotel with friendly service and plush rooms.
Radisson SAS, Šiaulių 28, Klaipėda, tel: (46) 490 800, www.radissonsas.com Five-star luxury. A fitness room and free Internet access are an added bonus.
Mama Rosa Villa, Jūratės 28a, Palanga, tel: (460) 48 581, www.mamarosa.lt

This classically styled villa is ideal for a romantic break.

MID-RANGE
Aribe, Bangu 17a, Klaipėda, tel: (46) 490 940, www.aribe.lt Modern 15-room hotel at the heart of Klaipėda Old Town.
Vila Miško Namas, Pamario 11, Nida, tel/fax: (46) 952 290, www.miskonamas.com An attractive villa with double rooms and apartments sleeping two to four people.
Litorina, Nidos-Smiltynės 19, Nida, tel: (469) 52 528, www.litorina-dubingiai.lt Pleasant hotel, 19 attractive double and triple rooms, sauna, tennis courts, café.
Alanga, S. Nėries 14, Palanga, tel: (460) 49 215, www.alanga.lt Hotel with 47 reasonably priced rooms.

BUDGET
Litinterp, Puodžių 17, Klaipėda, tel: (46) 410 644, www.litinterp.lt Agency offering B&B in Klaipėda.
Klaipėda Old Town Hostel, Butku Juzės 7-4, Klaipėda, tel: (46) 211 879, www.lithuanianhostels.org Clean, functional accommodation in a central location.

Nida Tourist Information Centre (see Useful Contacts) will book you a B&B.
Hotel Beržas, Minijos 2/Telšių 2, Plungė, tel/fax: (448) 56 840, http://berzas.service.lt Hotel with 12 good-value single and double rooms in the centre of town.

San Marino, (see Europa Royale). Upscale restaurant, modern European menu.
Mama Rosa Restaurant-Bar, (see Mama Rosa Villa). Good value salads, pasta, grilled meats and fresh fish.
Memelis, Zveju 4, Klaipėda, tel: (46) 403 040. Lashings of beer, hearty food and late opening hours. A hit with locals and visitors.

Klaipėda Tourist Information Centre, Turgaus 7, tel: (46) 412 186, www.klaipeda.lt
Nida Tourist Information Centre, Taikos 4, tel: (469) 52 345, www.visitneringa.com
Palanga Tourist Information Centre, Kretingos 1, tel: (460) 48 811, www.palangatic.lt
Curonian Spit National Park, www.nerija.lt

KLAIPĖDA	J	F	M	A	M	J	J	A	S	O	N	D
AVERAGE TEMP. °C	-2	-2	0	5	10	14	16	16	13	8	3	0
AVERAGE TEMP. °F	28	27	33	41	51	58	62	62	56	48	39	32
RAINFALL mm	50	31	39	36	39	56	74	83	89	80	90	68
RAINFALL in	2.0	1.2	1.5	1.4	1.5	2.2	2.9	3.3	3.5	3.1	3.5	2.7
DAYS OF RAINFALL	19	15	15	12	12	12	13	14	16	16	19	20

4
Inland Lithuania

Inland Lithuania is often missed out completely by tourists keen to visit the capital and then make a quick dash out to the country's coastline. Both, of course, have their merits, but it is well worth taking time to explore the rest of one of Europe's **least explored** countries.

Even within easy reach of Vilnius there is the historic gem of **Trakai**. Further layers of history can be uncovered in **Kaunas**, a city not at all content to accept the 'second city' tag. Kaunas indeed these days has direct budget airline flight connections to a number of European cities, meaning it is opening up for short breaks.

Delve further afield and you are really off the beaten track and you will need your own wheels to get about. Half the fun is just cruising around the countryside weaving past **seemingly endless fields** and **thick forests**, discovering as you go **forgotten villages** and rambling old churches. Other highlights include the remarkable **Hill of the Three Crosses** and the towns of **Druskininkai** and **Šiauliai**. The best of Lithuania's abundant countryside is on show in its trio of national parks at **Aukštaitija**, **Dzūkija** and **Žemaitija**, with walking trails, a wealth of flora and fauna to discover and oddities like a nuclear missile station that stands out as a Cold War anachronism.

TRAKAI ★★★
Trakai is the sort of historical creation that Walt Disney could only dream of emulating. Just a half-hour's drive from Vilnius this island bolthole was once the seat of Grand Duke Gediminas. You will never forget your first sight of the island

DON'T MISS

★★★ **Trakai:** one of Lithuania's most iconic images.
★★★ **Hill of Crosses:** an important religious site.
★★ **Kaunas:** Lithuania's vibrant second city impresses with its varied entertainment and dining scene, as well as some old buildings and quirky museums.
★★ **Žemaitija National Park:** see the secretive nuclear silos of the Soviet army.

Opposite: *Trakai Castle looks at its best when admired from the water with tour boats, rowing boats and yachts all on hand to open up the postcard perfect views.*

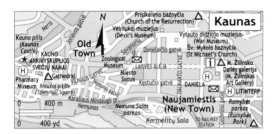

as you ramble down through the newer village (if you are hungry on the way try *kibinas*, the local meaty pastry that will keep you going) and the orange towers loom into view.

The island is accessible across two wooden walkways and you can also hire a rowing boat to get a unique view of the fortifications. In summer a tour boat runs from the castle out across the lake. The castle complex was a virtual ruin until the 1960s when the socialist-era authorities conjured up an unlikely renaissance with the red-brick castle rebuilt as close to the original design as possible. Inside museum exhibits tell its colourful story, but half the fun is just rambling around exploring the various rooms and walkways and, of course, that unforgettable approach. Open daily 10:00–19:00 in summer, daily 10:00–17:00 in winter.

KAUNAS **

Kaunas may only be Lithuania's second largest city, but this ambitious industrial hub at the confluence of the **Neris** and **Nemunas** rivers is not content to play second fiddle. The charming Old Town and increasingly lively new town boast a number of worthwhile sights, and then there are the city's numerous green spaces. Gone are the days of communist-era privations as these days Kaunas overflows with cafés and restaurants and a large local student population helps propel the nightlife scene.

Kaunas is not short on sights and thankfully most of them are housed on the plain where the old and new towns unfurl towards the Neris and Nemunas rivers on the western edge of the city.

Churches

To get an idea of the layout of Kaunas, the frankly bizarre mega **Prisikėlimo bažnyčia** (Church of the Resurrection) is the place. Looking more like a Willy Wonka factory than a church it nevertheless provides a bird's-eye view of the town. Get up there on the newly restored funicular at the north end of Mickevičiaus.

Walk down the hill and check out another striking church, **Šv. Mykolo bažnyčia** (St Michael's Church), which heralds the start of Laisvės. Lifeblood Laisvės takes in a mix of architectural styles and there will usually also be a stream of people as you head along in search of the Old Town. Laisvės's concrete pavement soon gives way to Vilniaus's cobbles and rambling old Gothic and Baroque architecture. Vilniaus eventually spills out into **Rotušės aikštė**, the Town Hall Square. The eponymous edifice hangs high above the scene and gives away its former role as a church.

Museums

As Lithuania's cultural and spiritual heart, Kaunas is also home to a sprinkling of excellent museums. The most bizarre has to be the **Velniukai muziejus** (Devil's Museum). This has around 2000 evil figures gathered from around the world by artist Antanas Zmuidzinavičius. Open Tuesday–Sunday 11:00–17:00, closed Monday.

The **Vytauto didžiojo muziejus** (War Museum) is an essential stop too, for the insight it provides into the country's turbulent history, but also for the ravaged clothes of the two local pilots (Steponas Darius and Stasys Girėnas) who famously perished trying to fly from the USA to Kaunas in 1923. Open Wednesday–Sunday 11:00–17:00, closed Monday and Tuesday.

Kauno Pilis

Another unmissable site is **Kauno pilis** (Kaunas Castle), a 14th-century fortress that has today been crowned with a rather fetching glass roof. It was the biggest castle complex in the Baltics when it opened and it is easy to peel back the centuries rambling around its ruins and rugged walls.

> **ŽEMAITIJA ART MUSEUM**
>
> This cultural temple housed in a Renaissance palace is not the sort of oasis that you would expect to find by the national park. The exhibits are not exactly earth shattering, but if you are passing by stop to check out the folk art and totem poles. Look out too for the Bechstein grand piano that used to belong to the renowned Lithuanian composer Mikalojus Čiurlionis, who lived here as a teenager when the palace was a music school.

Below: *St Michael's Church is the focus of any walk along Kaunas's pedestrianized main street.*

Pažaislio Vienuolynas

Located on the outskirts of Kaunas, the **Pažaislio vienuolynas** (Pažaislis Monastery) is on the itinerary of numerous tour operators. The best time to visit this beautiful and dramatic 17th-century Italian Baroque building is during the Pažaislis Music Festival, which brings classical music to the site during June, July and August.

OTHER PLACES TO VISIT
Druskininkai *

If you want to really relax after pounding Vilnius's or Kaunas's cobbles then make a beeline for the old spa town of **Druskininkai**. The healing properties of the local water are legendary and were recognized by royal decree as far back as the 18th century. The bubbling spring water is said to aid a variety of respiratory illnesses and also helps with stress conditions. The resort still attracts those in search of a cure for their various ailments, though the treatments are no longer free as they were for patients during Soviet times. Local legend has it that the waters are also spot-on for curing a hangover, handy if you have overdone it on the local beer.

Much of the town these days is modern and faceless, though a crumble of old spa buildings hint at the grander times. If you are in the mood for a mud bath or a massage don't expect a soothing, pampered luxury hotel spa experience; treatments here are definitely of the no-frills, medicinal variety.

Grūto Parkas *

This bizarre communist 'theme park' is laden with the sort of old Soviet-era statues that have disappeared from the rest of the old Eastern bloc. Lenin and Stalin live on in the **Grūto parkas** (most of the statues here are originals) just a 90-minute bus ride from Vilnius. It is kitsch but fascinating, especially for those who lived in Europe during the Cold War days when the reality of communist invasion was an all too real threat. The park was deeply controversial when it opened in 2001 and was quickly dubbed 'Stalin World', with many people seeing it as a crude attempt to make money rather than preserve history. Whatever the original motives, it has indeed served to preserve a fascinating period of history, which the people of the Baltics are still themselves trying to process. Open daily 09:00–18:00 in summer, 09:00–17:00 in winter.

Šiauliai

Šiauliai grew to prominence as far back as the 16th century as a major hub on the trading route between today's Kaliningrad and Rīga. Little of the charming old core remains after serious bombardment by Soviet tanks and artillery during World War II; however, some of the reconstruction has been surprisingly sensitive.

Museums worth checking out include the **Fotografijos muziejus** (Photography Museum), the **Radio ir TV muziejus** (Radio and Television Museum) and the **Dviračių muziejus** (Cycling Museum), the latter notable for its eclectic display of Vairas bikes. Vairas, the local manufacturer, was the Soviet Union's number one bicycle producer and is still going strong today, with the company having diversified into producing mountain bikes and even prams. All open Tuesday–Sunday 10:00–18:00, closed Monday.

Krijžų Kalnas ★★★

For some religious-minded visitors the **Krijžų kalnas** (Hill of Crosses) is the number one attraction in the country outside Vilnius – this unique sight should be unmissable for everyone. Around 10km (6 miles) out of Šiauliai rises the Jurgaičiai hill on which the crosses spike up. The site is swathed in some mystery, but most recent research suggests there used to be a wooden fort here that was levelled by the all-conquering Teutonic Knights. It seems to have held a special place in the hearts of Lithuanian Catholics ever since. In the 19th century the crosses became intertwined with resistance to increasingly bloody Tsarist rule and again it was against Russia that the crosses were erected in the 20th century when victims of the Siberian gulags were commemorated on the hillside.

By the 1960s the Soviets had lost their patience and ripped the site apart, banning the erection of any more crosses, though no matter how many times they tried to clear the site, back came the crosses in a standoff that came to

---

ZERVYNOS

The lovely little village of Zervynos, which is located within the boundaries of the Dzūkija National Park, consists of dozens of old farmsteads, which boast well-preserved examples of traditional wooden architecture. The youth hostel is a handy place to stay and they can advise on local walking trails as well as arrange canoe trips along the scenic Ūla river. On All Souls' Day the local people light fires in the Zervynos cemetery.

Below: *The Hill of the Crosses has a special place in the hearts and minds of Lithuanians and usually leaves a moving impression on visiting tourists too.*

symbolize Lithuanian resistance against rule from Moscow. Today it is impossible to count the thick forest of crosses, which form a moving site no matter your religious beliefs.

NATIONAL PARKS

Lithuania is blessed with some of the least spoilt landscapes and flora and fauna in Europe, and perhaps the best way of experiencing inland Lithuania's countryside is by visiting one of a trio of national parks:

Aukštaitijos Nacionalinis Parkas **

Glaciers may have formed the dramatic scenery of the much-loved **Aukštaitija nacionalinis parkas** (Aukštaitija National Park), but it was not protected as a national park until the 1970s. As with much of the country, a lot of the territory is covered in thick layers of pine forest, but it is also dotted with a sprinkling of little lakes. The best way to appreciate the park's scenery is to hike up to Ledakalnis, a small hill from where you can see a string of lakes, including the park's deepest lake, **Lake Tauragnas**. Look out here for golden eagles swooping around the treetops, as the park is one of the best places in the Baltics to view this mighty predator.

Man has made his own impressions on the landscape and there are dozens of small villages inside the park's sprawling boundaries. Cycling and walking are both good ways of getting around the park, but you can also indulge in a spot of canoeing and you can even camp within the park for a real back-to-nature experience.

Dzūkijos Nacionalinis Parkas **

This vast park covers over 500km² (193 sq miles) of protected land, much of it covered with thick pine forest, so breathe in deeply here to feel at one with the world again. The **Dzūkijos nacionalinis parkas** (Dzūkija National Park) is split up into a number of different nature reserves, with perhaps the most interesting the Čepkeliai Nature Reserve, which protects a large marshland that teems with bird life. The best way of getting around the park is with a bike, though there are also numerous walking trails. Follow the locals here in season to join the orgy of wild mushroom and berry picking, though be very careful what you pick as not all of it is safe to eat.

Žemaitijos Nacionalinis Parkas **

Spread across 200km² (77 sq miles) is the wilderness that is **Žemaitijos nacionalinis parkas** (Žemaitija National Park), home to the glacial Lake Plateliai, with its collage of seven islands. The highlight for many visitors from the Cold War generation is the **Soviet missile base**, which until independence was firmly off limits to even the local villagers.

Visiting this fascinating site is a surreal experience. You are led around by a bright-faced local student bedecked in an old Soviet-era costume who chirpily shows you the silos where missiles were once trained on targets all over Western Europe. While your imagination may already be running wild, wait until you descend below ground to unearth the missile chambers.

The dense smell of rocket fuel still fills the air in a dark netherworld that feels like the set from a James Bond movie. You dip your head to clunk between the various rooms where once Soviet troops wiled away the hours awaiting the fateful order to launch that thankfully never came. Various old bits and bobs of memorabilia are dotted around, but the real power is just in what this place is. Able-bodied visitors can squeeze up a narrow passage to stare right down the barrel of the gun, as it were, into one of the huge missile silos. Ask at the national park office for details of guided tours.

FESTIVALS IN LITHUANIA

March • **Kino Pavasaris Film Festival, Vilnius**
(www.kinopavasaris.lt)
April • **Kaunas Jazz**
(www.kaunasjazz.lt)
July • **Sea Festival, Klaipėda**
Bringing a carnival atmosphere to the city streets and sailing boats to the coast.
July • **Thomas Mann Festival, Nida**
Chamber music
July–August • **Pažaislis Music Festival, Kaunas**
Classical music
(www.pazaislis.lt)
August • **Trakai Festival**
Opera and classical music
October • **International Festival of Modern Dance, Kaunas, Alytus and Vilnius**
(www.dancefestival.lt)

Below: *Use your imagination to conjure up James Bond adventures and Cold War terror at the old nuclear missile base in the Žemaitija National Park.*

Inland Lithuania at a Glance

May–September is the best time to visit inland Lithuania when there are eight or nine hours of sunshine a day and days are pleasantly warm. At this time the country's second city, Kaunas, comes alive with street cafés and outdoor events. If you're visiting early or late in the season then you will need some warm clothing, as temperatures plummet after dark. Average temperatures fall below freezing in December, January and February.

Rail: Kaunas can be reached by train from Vilnius and Klaipėda. Regular trains run from the capital to Trakai.
Road: Long-distance **buses** link Kaunas to various towns and cities, including Šiauliai, Klaipėda and Vilnius. Trakai is a 45-minute bus ride from the capital.

The historic cores of Kaunas and Šiauliai are easily navigable by **foot**, as is Druskininkai. City **buses** and **taxis** are on hand for journeys further afield. To make the most of the national parks and to easily get between inland destinations you will need your own transport.

LUXURY
Daniela, A Mickevičiaus 28, Kaunas, tel: (37) 321 505,

fax: (37) 321 632, www.danielahotel.lt Free Wi-Fi, modern refurbished rooms (complete with plasma screen TVs) and an on-site restaurant tempt at the centrally located Daniela.
Apvalaus Stalo Klubas Hotel, Karaimų 53A, Trakai, tel: (528) 55 595, fax: (528) 51 760, www.asklubas.lt If you are feeling romantic then make a beeline for this elegant boutique hotel that looks over the lakes and castle at Trakai. The hotel also has a sauna, Jacuzzi, pizzeria and fine-dining restaurant.
Šaulys, Vasario 16-osios 40, Šiauliai, tel: (41) 520 812, www.saulys.lt The town's best hotel has 39 modern single, double and triple rooms, two apartments, its own swimming pool and restaurant.

MID-RANGE
Žaliakalnio Viešbutis, Žemaičių 31, Kaunas, tel: (37) 321 412, fax: (37) 733 769, www.greenhillhotel.lt Spectacular views over Kaunas's old and new towns, free Internet access and public spaces adorned with ever-changing art exhibitions more than compensate for this hotel's slightly dubious location – it is a huge concrete monstrosity adjacent to a strip club.
Trasilis, Gedimino 26, Trakai, tel: (528) 51 588, fax: (528) 51 589, www.trasalis.lt Added extras like a water slide, spa, billiards and bowling make

this modern hotel complex 3km (2 miles) from the centre of town a good choice.
Turnė, Rūdės 9, Šiauliai, tel: (41) 500 150, fax: (41) 429 238, www.turne.lt Offers modern doubles, triples and suites in a location that is handy for both the bus and train stations. The hotel also has a decent restaurant. If they are full ask about the nearby Turnė Guesthouse.
Regina, T. Kosciuskos 3, Druskininkai, tel: (313) 59 060, fax: (313) 59 061, www.regina.lt This lovely three-star hotel has 40 modern rooms. Its three de luxe rooms are big enough to accommodate a family of four.
Draugystė Sanatorija, Kreves 7, Druskininkai, tel: (313) 52 378. Established in 1962, the sanatorium's name translates as 'friendship'. Rates (from around €25 per person) include lodgings, food and access to some spa facilities; a good value option.

BUDGET
Litinerp, Gedimino St 28-7, Kaunas, tel: (37) 228 718, fax: (37) 425 120, www.litinterp.lt Agency offering B&B in Kaunas.
Kauno Arkivyskupijos Svečių Namai, Rotušės 21, Kaunas, tel. (37) 322-597, fax: (37) 320-090, http://kaunas.lcn.lt/sveciunamai Owned by the church this pleasant guesthouse offers 21 reasonably

Inland Lithuania at a Glance

priced and well-finished rooms just off Town Hall Square. Satellite TV and free Internet are added bonuses. No breakfast.

Salos, Kranto 50, Trakai, tel: (528) 53 990, fax: (528) 53 991, www.salos.lt A hotel, restaurant and nightclub in one, Salos tends to attract a younger clientele. With just 10 well-appointed rooms, though, this is a good budget option.

The **Tourist Information Centres** (see Useful Contacts) in Šiauliai and Druskininkai can help you arrange private accommodation.

Avilys, Vilniaus 34, Kaunas, tel: (37) 207 552, www.avilys.lt Head here for this microbrewery's organic honey-infused ale and unusual culinary delights like beer soup.
Medžiotojų Užeiga, Rotušės 10, Kaunas, tel: 320 956, www.medziotojai.lt Ideal if you're hankering after rich game or other hearty Lithuanian meat dishes.
Apvalaus Stalo Klubas, (see Apvalaus Stalo Klubas hotel). Panoramic castle and lake views and a waterside summer terrace are reason enough to dine at Apvalaus Stalo Klubas. The food on a menu that combines Mediterranean and Lithuanian influences does not disappoint either.
Café Kaukas, Tilžės 144, Šiauliai. Good for light meals

during the day and more nefarious nightlife by night.
Café Alka, Veisiejų 13b, Druskininkai, tel: (616) 12 965, www.kavinealka.lt This alpine-style lodge-cum-café-bar has been entertaining visitors for over 30 years with the assortment of weird and wonderful woodcarvings that decorate both its exterior and interior. It also has a pleasant woodland location and outside seating area.

Kaunas has the kind of shopping scene that you might expect to find in a city of its size. The bulk of the city's shops and souvenir stalls are located on the central strip that marks the boundary between the old and new towns. **Vilniaus** street is an essential stop for souvenir hunters, while larger shops dot **Savanorių** street. In the summer months market traders also peddle their wares on **Laisvės** street.

Walking tours of Kaunas are organized by the **Tourist Information Centre**, the

Kauno Saitas Travel Agency. Various agencies in Vilnius also organize day trips by bus to destinations like **The Hill of Crosses**, **Trakai**, **Grūto Parkas**, **Kaunas**, **Pažaislis Monastery** and the **Aukštaitija National Park**. Vilnius City Tour (tel: (5) 261 5558, www.vilniuscitytour.com) is one company that offers excursions like these from the capital.

Trakai Tourist Information Centre, Vytauto 69, tel: (528) 51 934, www.trakai.lt
Kaunas Tourist Information Centre, Laisvės 36, tel: (37) 323 436, http://visit.kaunas.lt
Druskininkai Tourist Information Centre, Gardino 3, tel: (313) 60 800, www.druskininkai.lt
Šiauliai Tourist Information Centre, Vilniaus 213, tel: (41) 523 110, www.siauliai.lt/tic
Grūto Parkas, www.grutoparkas.lt
Aukštaitija National Park, www.anp.lt
Dzūkija National Park, www.dzukijosparkas.lt
Žemaitija National Park, www.zemaitijosnp.lt

KAUNAS	J	F	M	A	M	J	J	A	S	O	N	D
AVERAGE TEMP. °C	-3	-3	1	6	12	15	17	16	12	7	2	-1
AVERAGE TEMP. °F	26	26	34	44	55	60	63	62	54	45	36	29
RAINFALL mm	39	31	35	42	55	69	80	78	56	45	53	47
RAINFALL in	1.5	1.2	1.4	1.7	2.2	2.7	3.1	3.1	2.2	1.8	2.1	1.9
DAYS OF RAINFALL	18	14	14	13	13	13	14	13	15	15	17	19

5
Rīga

Since Latvia's break with the Soviet Union in 1991 the country's cosmopolitan capital has gone from strength to strength. EU accession and NATO membership in 2004 cemented Rīga's position in the European family and saw an accompanying influx in the number of tourists. When it comes to foreign visitor numbers Rīga continues to set a new record each year.

The capital, though, hasn't always had it so good, and its informative museums recount the routine sackings and occupations that have shaped its development over more than 800 years. Arguably, the 20th century was the most devastating for Rīga, with the Soviet occupation of 1944–91 leaving a legacy of monstrous housing estates and some ugly architectural souvenirs.

Any lingering images of communist-era deprivations that first-time visitors may have are soon put paid to in a city where modern tower blocks, renovated historical buildings, stylish mobile phone-touting locals and chic bars and cafés stand side by side.

Rīga **Old Town** is an attractive maze of winding cobbled streets, grand squares and vaulting church spires nestling on the right bank of the River Daugava. This historic core, which has remained largely unchanged since medieval times, and the rich collection of **Jugendstil** (Germanic Art Nouveau) architecture in the **New Town** secured Rīga a well-deserved place on the **UNESCO World Heritage List** in 1997. Throw in a big-city buzz and it is perhaps unsurprising that many visitors to the Baltic States declare that the Latvian capital is their favourite city in the region.

Opposite: *Rīga's Old Town is these days flooded with welcoming cafés and bars.*

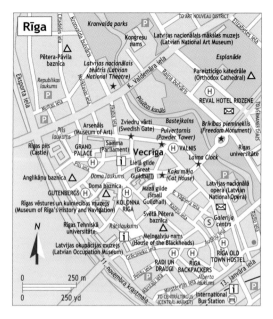

OLD TOWN

Vecrīga (Old Rīga) can easily be explored on foot, as it is pancake flat and there are myriad cafés, bars and restaurants on hand for a quick pit stop along the way.

Pils Laukums **

The principal attraction on **Pils laukums** (Castle Square) is **Rīgas pils** (Riga Castle), a multi-functional building that is home to the country's president and two museums.

In the **Latvijas ārzemju mākslas muzejs** (Latvian Museum of Foreign Art) you will be treated to the country's largest collection of international art. Open Tuesday–Sunday 11:00–17:00, closed Monday.

The **Latvijas vēstures muzejs** (Latvian History Museum), meanwhile, traces the country's evolution through a series of archaeological, ethnographic and historic artefacts. Open Monday–Saturday 11:00–19:00 and Sunday 10:00–13:00.

Doma Laukums ***

Continuing south along Pils iela brings you to the magnificent **Doma laukums** (Cathedral Square) where **Rīgas doms** or **Doma baznīca** (Riga Cathedral) awaits. One of the city's most iconic and most visited attractions dates back to the early 13th century, when Albert von Buxhoeveden became this ecclesiastical masterpiece's first bishop. The cathedral's attractive façade is an intriguing mix of Romanesque and Gothic architecture. Open Tuesday–Friday 13:00–18:00, Saturday 10:00–14:00, closed Sunday–Monday.

Rātslaukums ★★★

The last in the trio of squares is the elegant **Rātslaukums** (Town Hall Square), a painstaking post World War II reconstruction. Here you will find Rīga's main tourist information centre, the city's Town Hall and the impossibly ornate House of the Blackheads. St Peter's Church is located just east of the square.

Although the **Melngalvju nams** (House of the Blackheads) looks old (the original was constructed in 1344), this impressive reconstruction, an 800th anniversary gift to Rīga's citizens, dates from 2001. Incredibly, the Soviets razed the original rather than using the ruins (a casualty of World War II) to rebuild. Dismissed by the brutal occupying power as an example of decadent 'Germanic' architecture, today's structure is an attractive showcase of Dutch Renaissance and Gothic design. Open Tuesday–Sunday 10:00–17:00, closed Monday.

Dedicated to Rīga's patron saint, **Svētā Pētera baznīca** (St Peter's Church) is a striking red-brick edifice, characteristic of the Baltic region. Erected at the turn of the 15th century to replace a dilapidated wooden structure, the church's original timber spire (once the highest in Europe) was destroyed during the war by either German shelling or the retreating Russian army. Today's voluminous steel replica, which stands 122m (400ft) tall, dates from 1973 and offers spectacular 360° views from 72m (236ft) above the city. Open Tuesday–Sunday 10:00–18:00, closed Monday.

Latvijas Okupācijas Muzejs ★★★

Much maligned as an architectural blot on Rīga's attractive Old Town landscape, the oblong black box that houses the **Latvijas okupācijas muzejs** (Latvian Occupation Museum), if viewed in another way, is fittingly austere. One of the city's most illuminating and compelling museums takes visitors on an often harrowing journey back in time to World War II, when first the German and then the

SIGHTSEEING TIPS

Rīga can often be very busy at weekends with stag and hen parties, so if you wany to enjoy a quieter time then consider visiting midweek. As the centre is so compact there is no need to book a tour – you can just guide yourself around the flat core. Also, make at least one trip across the Daugava River, where you will enjoy the best views of the Old Town shimmering across the water.

Below: *Doma laukums is at the heart of the Old Town and is home to the city's impressive cathedral.*

Soviet occupation of the city sounded the knell of the dark times to come. The museum's story, as you might expect, ends with hard-won Latvian independence in 1991. Open daily 11:00–18:00 May–September, Tuesday–Sunday 11:00–17:00, closed Monday October–April.

Strēlnieku Piemineklis

Outside the Occupation Museum the **Strēlnieku pieminek-lis** (Latvian Riflemen Monument) is a memorial to the Latvian Red Riflemen, many of whom went on to become Lenin's bodyguards. The long-term future of the statue is hotly contested, with supporters arguing that it is a valid testimony to the bravery of Latvian soldiers who sacrificed their lives during World War II. Its opponents decry it as a celebration of the communist regime that oppressed Latvia for almost 50 years.

Below: *The Occupation Museum provides an illuminating and moving insight into both the German and Russian occupations that blighted much of Latvian life for long periods of the 20th century.*

Pulvertornis **

Not only is the **Pulvertornis** (Powder Tower) – a sturdy red-brick fortification that has helped see off would-be invaders during its 700-year history – one of Rīga's oldest buildings, but it also houses the **Latvijas kara muzejs** (Latvian War Museum). Before popping into the museum take time to note the cannonballs wedged into its exterior walls (a gift from the Russians). Open Wednesday–Sunday 10:00–18:00, closed Monday May–September; Wednesday–Sunday 10:00–17:00, closed Monday October–April.

Centrāltirgus *

Brimming with local colour, the largest market in the Baltic States is the place to visit if you want a feel for shopping rituals that have gone unchanged for more than 70 years. Spread out over four former Zeppelin hangars (when it opened in 1930 all five

hangars were occupied by stalls), Rīga's **Centrāltirgus** (Central Market) is the place to stock up on fruit, vegetables, bread and dairy products, with farmers from all over the country peddling their wares here. Over the last few years some souvenirs have also been creeping in. It is very much the old Latvia.

Brīvības Piemineklis ★★

On the cusp of the Old and New towns you will find the **Brīvības piemineklis** (Freedom Monument), one of Latvia's most iconic attractions. Milda, as she is also known, holds a special place in the hearts of Rīgans and Latvians everywhere. Erected back in 1935, this vaulting shrine to Latvian nationalism emerged, miraculously, unscathed from more than four decades of Soviet rule. The young woman holds three stars, which symbolize the country's historical regions of Vidzeme, Latgale and Kurzeme, above her head, while statues around the base depict Latvians toiling (through battle, song and work) for their independence. The foot of the statue is often adorned with flowers in a poignant reminder of those Rīgans who in a defiant stance against the communist regime dared to do the same. If caught, the perpetrators were, somewhat harshly, deported to Siberia.

NEW TOWN

Home to a number of bars and restaurants, including raffish watering holes, the trendy Voodoo nightclub and the Skyline Bar (a must visit on any itinerary), Rīga's New Town, save its magnificent Art Nouveau quarter, is relatively low on sights.

Art Nouveau ★★★

The broad **Elizabetes iela** (Elizabeth Street) is at the heart of Rīga's Art Nouveau district, where an exploration of Strēlnieku iela, Alberta iela and Elizabetes iela itself (a gentle low-level stroll) is rewarded with some of the most impressive Jugendstil façades in the world. This architectural style was in vogue from the turn of the 19th century through to the outbreak of war in 1914. Highlights include the Stockholm School of Economics at **Strēlnieku iela** 4a and the adjacent Rīga Graduate School of Law. Together

---

JĀNIS ČAKSTE

Čakste is still revered within Latvia today as the first president of an independent Latvia. Born in the country in 1859, he served in the Russian parliament, the Duma, where he pushed for greater Latvian autonomy. His wish came true when he took on the role of leader of the Latvian government in 1918, becoming the official president in 1922. His success was recognized when he was re-elected in 1925, only for him to die in office two years later.

AT THE MARKET

Rīga's Central Market is a real must-see (see this page). Some tourist-orientated items have crept in over the last few years to accompany the collage of food and drink stalls. Don't be afraid to bargain here even if some of the sellers do look a bit fearsome. Market stalls line the Old Town selling souvenirs and again do not be afraid to bargain especially if you are buying more than one item. The old walking away trick can also pay dividends.

ART NOUVEAU WALK

Rīga boasts arguably the most impressive collection of elaborate 19th-century Jugendstil (German Art Nouveau) architecture in the world. A walk along Kalpalka iela, which heads west off Brīvības (just north-east of the Freedom Monument), Strēlnieku iela, Alberta iela, Antonijas iela and Elizabetes iela will take you past the most ornate examples. Highlights include the work of Russian-born Mikhail Eisenstein on Strēlnieku and Alberta.

they epitomize the architectural style of Mikhail Eisenstein (1867–1921) whose signature geometric lines, rooftop statues, imposing busts and ornate wrought-iron balconies are stamped all over this part of the city.

The Russian-born architect's masterpieces are also the standout on **Alberta iela**, where the residential apartments at numbers 2, 2a, 4, 6 and 8 are adorned with dragons, sphinxes and attractive rooftop arches.

On Elizabetes iela itself many tourists would argue that the **Skyline Bar**, whose floor-to-ceiling windows offer spectacular panoramas over Old and New Rīga from the 26th floor of the Reval Hotel Latvija, is the main attraction. The hotel's nightclub, Voodoo, is also one of the city's hottest nightlife tickets.

GREEN SPACES
Bastejkalns *

This leafy central park marks the boundary between Old and New Rīga. **Bastejkalns** (Bastion Hill) is popular with locals and visitors alike who come here to meet friends, bask in the summer sunshine or to take a walk along the banks of the **Pilsētas kanāls** (City Canal). It is also enshrined in the national consciousness for an altogether more sinister reason. Back in January 1991, when Soviet troops moved in to try and prevent Latvia from break-ing away from Moscow's control, five innocent Latvians were shot dead – including a student and two cameramen. Today, evocative memorial stones, nestling quietly among the trees, commemorate this tragic event.

Kronvalda

Immediately north of Bastejkalns and Krisjana Valdemāra iela this quiet little park also reclines by the City Canal. With few distractions bar the opulent **Latvijas nacionālais teātris** (Latvian National Theatre)

Below: *The Freedom Monument is a deeply symbolic icon that is at the heart of both Rīga and Latvia emotionally, historically and spiritually.*

and sculptures of two Latvian legends – composer Alfrēds Kalniņš and writer Rūdolfs Blaumanis – this is a good place to unwind.

Esplanāde ★★

Located just east of Bastejkalns, the **Esplanāde** is a pleasant and neatly landscaped place, with colourful flowerbeds and manicured lawns. The Pareizticīgo katedrāle and the Latvijas nacionālais mākslas muzejs, though, are the main tourist drawcards.

Above: *Ornate Germanic Art Nouveau architecture is one of Rīga's highlights.*

Dedicated to Alexander Nevsky and named after a 13th-century Russian prince championed as a folk hero amongst Rīga's Russian population, the **Pareizticīgo katedrāle** (Orthodox Cathedral, a gleaming onion-domed house of prayer (there are five domes), dates back to the late 19th century.

Latvia's art history unfolds in the expansive collection at the **Latvijas nacionālais mākslas muzejs** (Latvian National Art Museum), which incorporates over 50,000 pieces dating from the middle of the 18th century to the end of World War II. Notable works include pieces by renowned Latvian artists like Janis Rozentāls, Ludolfs Liberts, Biruta Baumane and Vilhelms Purvītis. The opulent early 20th-century building that houses the museum is worth visiting in its own right. Open Monday 11:00–17:00, Wednesday 11:00–17:00, Thursday 11:00–19:00 and Friday–Sunday 11:00–17:00, closed Tuesday April to September; Wednesday–Sunday 11:00–17:00, closed Tuesday October to March.

Vērmanes Dārzs

Situated in the New Town to the southeast of Brīvības bulvāris, **Vērmanes dārzs** (Vērmanes Garden) overflows with local colour. This is the place where Rīgans come to laze over a novel or challenge their friends to a game of chess. A small outdoor theatre also hosts the odd summer concert or play

TAKE ME TO THE RIVER

Taking to the water is a great way to appreciate Rīga's drama. Which boats are running and who is running them seems to change as often as the seasons so ask at the tourist office for current details. Some hotels will also make bookings for you. Whoever you go with, have your camera at the ready as the Daugava opens up some great vistas of the city's spire-strewn skyline.

and there is a very good tea house in the park. A picture of calm, the park's history wasn't always so peaceful. In 1812, as Napoleon's troops advanced towards the city, Russian soldiers razed the residential houses that stood here before, in a desperate bid to protect Rīga from invasion.

DAUGAVA

An integral part of city life, the broad expanse of the River Daugava rushes through the city on its journey to the Baltic Sea. While every visitor sees the river, few have reason to cross it. During the warmer months the tour boats that ply its waters provide a unique vantage point from which to view **Vecrīga** (Old Rīga). Those who have found their sea legs can also make longer jaunts to Rīga's rambling port and the seaside resorts of Jūrmala. Trips leave from the pier at 11 Novembra Krastmala.

Rīgas TV Tornis *

Located on Zaķusala island in the middle of the Daugava River, the **Rīgas TV tornis** (Rīga TV Tower), a concrete structure on three legs, may not be Rīga's most attractive landmark, but it is worth making the journey from the Old Town. On a clear day the most compelling reason to come here is to admire the view from the observation tower, which elevates visitors 97m (318ft) above sea level. In the right weather it is possible to see ships in the Gulf of Rīga.

Below: *Bastejkalns Park is Rīga's favourite green lung with its sculptures, cafés and walkways.*

OUTSIDE THE CITY CENTRE
Latvijas Etnogrāfiskais Brīvdabas Muzejs **

Situated a good 10km (6 miles) east of Vecrīga the **Latvijas etnogrāfiskais brīvdabas muzejs** (Latvian Open-air Ethnographic Museum), which sheds light on 19th-century Latvian life, is well worth a visit. Highlights at this expansive woodland site include original timber buildings from around the country that were painstakingly dismantled before being reconstructed here. Open daily 10:00–17:00.

Mežaparks

The principal reason to visit the out-of-town **Mežaparks** (Forest Park) is to see the captive animals, including tigers, rhinos and penguins, at **Rīgas zoodārz** (Rīga National Zoo). This park is the location for many of the major Latvian song festivals. Open daily 10:00–16:00.

Pārdaugava

Few visitors venture onto the left bank of the Daugava River, but the **Pārdaugava** area of the city rewards exploration with the **Latvijas universitātes botāniskais dārzs** (Latvian University Botanical Garden), leafy parks, traditional fisherman houses, attractive churches, an early 20th-century water tower and old wooden cottages. The tourist office can help organize guided tours of Pārdaugava's key sights.

Salaspils *

One of the most sobering sights in Latvia is located 18km (12 miles) southeast of the capital. During World War II somewhere in the region of 100,000 innocent civilians were executed at the **Salaspils** concentration camp. At least 50% of the victims were Jewish.

The German forces attempted to eradicate the evidence of their terrible deeds as they retreated, so you won't find any gas chambers or residential barracks. Instead, the memorial park has a collection of oversized human statues whose Soviet triumphalist style doesn't really seem to do justice to the tragedy of Salaspils. Their existence, though, is another poignant reminder of the oppression experienced by the Latvian people for a large chunk of the 20th century, when all of the key decisions affecting their lives were made in Moscow.

Nearby, the **Rumbula Forest** is another tragic site, where around 28,000 Rīgan Jews were slain in just a week by the Nazis. It is said that only three people who arrived at the site actually escaped death. Today a memorial commemorates this mass murder.

USEFUL LATVIAN PHRASES

Labdien • hello/good day
Uz redzēšanos • goodbye
Lūdzu • please
Paldies • thank you
Cik? • how much?
Slimnīca • hospital
Lidosta • airport
Viens, viena • one
Divi, divas • two
Trīs • three
Četri • four
Pieci • five
Seši • six
Septiņi • seven
Astoņi • eight
Deviņi • nine
Desmit • 10
Simts • 100

Rīga at a Glance

Best Times to Visit

May–September, when days are pleasantly warm, is the best time to visit Rīga. At this time the city's vibrant café culture spills out into the streets. If you are visiting early or late in the season then don't forget to pack some warm clothing, as temperatures plummet after dark. Winters are cold but drier. January–March have the least rainfall.

Getting There

Air: Air Baltic fly to Rīga from Liepāja. Buses 22 and 22a run from the airport to the Old Town. Taxis also ply the airport route.
Rail: Direct trains link Rīga to Majori (Jūrmala), Rēzekne, Salaspils and Daugavpils.
Road: Myriad Latvian towns and cities have direct **buses** to Rīga. The capital is at the heart of the country's road network.

Getting Around

Central Rīga is easily navigable on **foot**. City **buses**, **trolleybuses, trams** and **taxis** also operate in the city. Buy bus and trolleybus tickets on board and tram tickets from news kiosks.

Where to Stay

Luxury
Grand Palace,
Pils 12, tel: (6704 4000,
fax: 6704 4001,
www.schlossle-hotels.com
A strong contender for Rīga's best hotel, this luxurious

abode housed in a historic building between Pils laukums and Doma laukums promises a first-class stay with all the frills.
Reval Hotel Latvija,
Elizabetes 55, tel: 6777 2222,
fax: 6777 2221,
www.revalhotels.com
This modern five-star hotel is renowned for the panoramic views from its Skyline Bar. Secure a similar view in one of the upper floor rooms.
Radisson SAS Daugava,
Kugu 24, tel: 6706 1111,
fax: 6706 1100,
www.riga.radissonsas.com
Located on the left bank of the River Daugava the best rooms at this first-rate hotel look back over the Old Town. For those who want to keep fit the property boasts a pool and gym.
Gutenbergs,
Doma laukums 1, tel: 6781 4090, fax: 6750 3326,
www.gutenbergs.lv
Combining old-world charm, modern elegance and an extremely central location, this is a good place to stay. The 5th floor rooftop terrace boasts great views.

Mid-range
Hotel Kolonna Rīga,
Tirgoņu 9, tel: 6735 8254,
fax: 6735 8255,
www.hotel.kolonna.com
The light and modern rooms at this boutique property are a pleasant contrast with the old building (a former merchant's

home) that houses them. Impress a loved one and book the penthouse – its windows overlook the Old Town roofs.
Elizabetes Nams,
Elizabetes 27, tel: 6750 9292,
fax: 6750 9291,
www.elizabetesnams.lv
A pleasant boutique hotel housed in an old wooden building, with idiosyncratic rooms and nice design touches.
City Hotel Bruņinieks,
Bruņinieku 6, tel: 6731 5140,
fax: 6731 4310,
www.cityhotel.lv
Its location 15 minutes from the Old Town and good-sized rooms ensure that this hotel is always busy. Added highlights include panoramic views from the 7th-storey restaurant and a sauna.
Radi un Draugi,
Mārstaļu 1/3, tel: 6782 0200,
fax: 6782 0202,
www.draugi.lv Another mid-range gem at the heart of the Old Town, Radi un Draugi has clean and comfortable singles, doubles, triples and junior suites.

Budget
Livonija,
Maskavas 32, tel: 6720 4180,
fax: 6720 4189,
www.hotellivonija.lv
Located southeast of the Central Market this motel is a brisk 15–20-minute walk from the Old Town. Trams stop outside.
Valnis,
Vaļņu 2, tel: 6721 3785.

Rīga at a Glance

These 'apartments' may be large and clean with refrigerators and private bathrooms, but don't expect too much from the Soviet-era décor; here you get what you pay for. The location, though, is hard to beat.

Rīga Backpackers, Mārstaļu 6, tel: 6722 9922, fax: 6722 1023, www.riga-backpackers.com Housed in a renovated old building at the heart of the Old Town, this hostel is a good budget option. Book early to bag one of the eight single, double or triple rooms. The two suites and apartment are slightly more expensive.

Rīga Old Town Hostel, Vaļnu 43, tel: 6722 3406, www.rigaoldtownhostel.lv More in keeping with hostel accommodation, the majority of beds at Rīga Old Town Hostel are in six- or 12-bed dorms; book ahead for the two double rooms.

WHERE TO EAT

Staburags, Caka 55, tel: 6729 9787. Thirst-quenching domestic beer and hearty Latvian food are the order of the day at this fun and reasonably priced restaurant.
Vincents, Elizabetes 16, tel: 6733 2830. Championed by many as Rīga's best restaurant, on a good night Vincents serves up decent food and has a pleasant ambience.
Soraksans, Miesnieku 12, tel:

6722 9068. If you find it hard to marry the notion of Korean cuisine with the Baltic States, you'll be pleasantly surprised. Platters of reasonably priced sushi are the highlight.
Zivju Restorāns Skonto, Vagnera 4, tel: 6721 6731. Those hankering after mouth-watering fish dishes should make a beeline for this excellent restaurant.
Bergs, Hotel Bergs, Elizabetes 83/85, tel: 6777 0900. Challenging Vincents for the city's gourmet crown, service and food are guaranteed to be of a high standard at the eponymous hotel's signature restaurant.

SHOPPING

Rīga's **Old Town** is flooded with boutique shops selling everything from amber to Soviet memorabilia. One typically Rīgan souvenir is **Rīgas Melnais Balzams** (Rīga Black Balzams), a lethal alcoholic drink whose herbal ingredients (apparently there are 24) give it an unpleasant bitter taste. Locals swear by its medicinal properties and mix it with soft drinks or pour it into coffee. In the

winter locals mix hot Black Balzams with blackcurrant juice and fresh fruit – great for colds.

TOURS AND EXCURSIONS

City **bus tours** pick up from the Opera House and a number of Rīga's hotels, while **walking tours** can be arranged at the tourist office. In season **Daugava river cruises** leave from 11 Novembra Krasmala. Organized bus excursions are also available to destinations like **Rundāle Palace**, **Sigulda** and **Jūrmala**.

USEFUL CONTACTS

Tourist Information Centre, 1-2 Rātslaukums 6, tel: 6703 7900, www.rigatourism.com
Rīga Airport, tel: 6720 7090, www.riga-airport.com
Air Baltic, Rīga Airport, tel: 6720 7777, www.air-baltic.com
Railway Station, Stacijas laukums, tel: 1181 or 6723 1181, www.ldz.lv
Bus Station, Prāga 1, tel: 900 0009, www.autoosta.lv
Sightseeing Tours of Rīga, tel: 6727 1915, www.sightseeing.lv

RĪGA	J	F	M	A	M	J	J	A	S	O	N	D
AVERAGE TEMP. °C	-3	-3	0	5	11	15	17	16	12	7	2	-1
AVERAGE TEMP. °F	26	26	33	42	53	60	63	62	54	45	37	29
RAINFALL mm	34	27	28	41	44	63	85	73	75	60	57	46
RAINFALL in	1.3	1.1	1.1	1.6	1.7	2.5	3.3	2.9	3.0	2.4	2.2	1.8
DAYS OF RAINFALL	20	17	15	14	11	14	13	13	14	15	21	22

6
Coastal Latvia

Latvia's coast is one of the country's best-kept secrets; well, from international tourists at least. Running almost 513km (330 miles) from **Ainaži** in the north to **Nida** (not to be confused with Nida in Lithuania) in the south and skirting both the **Baltic Sea** and its offshoot the **Gulf of Rīga**, coastal Latvia boasts a seemingly endless succession of white and golden sand beaches. Flanked by row upon row of pine trees, the sands are popular with Latvian families taking a dip during the summer.

Outside of the main summer months (June–August) even the most accessible beaches can be quiet, while those that lie away from the towns and cities, just off Latvia's coastal roads, are often deserted whatever the season. Some dismiss the Latvian coast as a cold, barren and windswept place, and while this may be true in the winter, its beaches are still a great place for an invigorating walk.

There is of course more to the coast than sand, and a visit to the region can incorporate everything from vibrant cities and historic villages, through to unusual museums, nature reserves and attractive monuments.

To the northwest of **Rīga** county the **Livonian Coast** was once the exclusive domain of the ethnic **Livs** (of which there are only around 100 today and it is thought that the Liv language is now spoken by just ten people). Much of the blustery shoreline, which ranks amongst Latvia's most dramatic seaside scenery, is protected within the **Slītere National Park**. To really explore Livonia, though, you'll need a car and nerves of steel, with many of its roads little more than rough loose stone or sand-covered tracks.

DON'T MISS

*** Cape Kolka: an impressive sight where the Gulf of Rīga crashes into the Baltic Sea.
** Slītere Lighthouse: get a bird's-eye view from the top and check out the photographs of other Latvian lighthouses.
** Ventspils: a city that is reinventing itself as it wakes up to its tourist potential.
** Liepāja: its grandeur may be faded but Liepāja boasts some striking architecture.
** Majori: laid-back and enjoyable coastal town.

Opposite: *A solitary boat sits bereft on a long and lovely stretch of Latvia's expansive Baltic coastline.*

JŪRMALA

Jūrmala, which means 'coast', is a collection of seaside villages that together boast a 33km (21-mile) stretch of Blue Flag-winning beaches.

Majori ★★

Jūrmala's tourism nucleus, **Majori**, is located just 20km (12 miles) southwest of Rīga and it is a popular weekend playground for city dwellers. Although a little frayed around the edges, the town boasts indulgent spas, improving hotels, a casino and a smattering of decent restaurants. Majori is also home to dozens of charming old wooden houses, a couple of museums and, of course, a wide expanse of pristine beach.

Get in touch with your cultural side at the **Jūrmalas pilsētas muzejs** (Jūrmala City Museum), which looks back at the resort's heyday, the evolution of spa tourism and the more recent investment in its rejuvenation. Open Tuesday–Sunday 11:00–17:00, closed Monday.

At the **Raiņa un Aspazijas memoriālā vasarnīca** (Rainas and Aspazija Summer House) you can learn about the lives and works of Latvian writers Janis Rainas (1865–1929) and Elza Rozenberga (1865–1943). Their holiday home-cum-museum gives you a feel for their lives through a collection of private belongings housed in one of the Jūrmala's signature wooden houses. A visit also gives you a chance to get inside one of the resort's timber cottages. Open Wednesday–Sunday 11:00–18:00, closed Monday and Tuesday.

For a truly relaxing visit to Majori book yourself a soothing massage or hydrotherapy treatment at either the **Alve Spa Centre**, the **Baltic Beach Hotel** or the **Hotel Jūrmala Spa**. More esoteric treatments include 40 minutes in the salt cave, and a romantic bath for two is on offer in the latter.

Lielupe

In the east of Jūrmala, **Lielupe** boasts historic wooden cottages which were the former homes of famous Latvians, including writer Ernests Birznieks-Upīts (1871–1960). Lielupe also has the region's biggest sand dune.

Dzintari

Continue on the cultural trail with a visit to **Dzintari**, the town whose name translates as 'amber', and its rather unusual museums: the **Museum of Prison History** and the **Museum of Old Machinery**. The former tells the story behind incarceration from the Middle Ages through to the present. Interestingly, the latter has a collection of transport from days gone by, including a car that belonged to the Russian Tsar Nicholas II. Check at the tourist office in Majori for current opening hours.

Bulduri

If the Majori spas have given you a taste for pampering, or the treatment prices at its up-market hotels have scared you off, then why not book a mud wrap, paraffin treatment or therapeutic massage at the Bulduri's **Amber Spa**.

Akvaparks Livu

Jūrmala's **Akvaparks Livu** (Nemo Water Park) is a water wonderland of slides, rapids and a wave pool. Modest in size when compared to the water parks of Mediterranean Europe, the Akvaparks, with its six waterslides, is one of the largest of its kind in this part of the continent.

LIVONIAN COAST
Cape Kolka ★★★

Take a bracing walk on the beach on a blustery day and watch the Baltic Sea and the Gulf of Rīga collide at **Cape Kolka**. It is really quite surreal to watch the waves travelling in opposite directions. The currents here are notorious, though, so confine your visit to the land.

Below: *Wooden architecture abounds in Jūrmala and attempts are being made to preserve it for future generations to enjoy after years of neglect during the Soviet occupation.*

Vaide

If you've got a penchant for horns and antlers then it's worth popping into the village of **Vaide**. Otherwise innocuous, this small hamlet boasts what has to be one of Latvia's most unusual museums: the **Ragu kolekcija** (Horn Collection). Erratic opening hours.

Mazirbe

The village of **Mazirbe** is at the centre of the efforts to preserve Liv culture, and is home to both the **Lībiešu tautas nams** (Livonian Cultural Centre) and an eye-catching wooden memorial. The cultural centre, housed in a renovated Livonian home, dispenses local tourist information, hosts educational events and houses various exhibitions about Liv life. Continue beyond Mazirbe's residential heart and you will find the kind of attractive white sand beaches that are characteristic of the Livonian coast.

Slītere Lighthouse ★★

Arguably the most striking set piece in the **Slītere National Park**, the **Slītere Lighthouse** is certainly its most mainstream tourist attraction. Strangely, this handsome red lighthouse is not located on the sea, but rises up a few kilometres inland instead. For a small fee you can climb to the viewing deck and soak up 360° panoramas over vast swathes of pine forests and the Baltic Sea. A photographic exhibition on a lower floor gives you the chance to admire other Latvian lighthouses. You can also join a guided nature walk into the forests around the lighthouse.

THE REST OF THE KURZEME COAST
Ventspils ★★

A city at the heart of Latvia's oil industry, **Ventspils** is a reasonably affluent place, with around 10% of Russia's crude oil transiting through this busy Baltic port. Some critics have, somewhat unkindly, suggested that some of Ventspils's riches could be used to renovate its faded, in parts, Old Town. Investment in the city, though, is ongoing and Ventspils is emerging as one of the country's most popular destinations for day-tripping Latvians. A key component of its success is a clean-up operation that transformed Ventspils's city beach from one of the most polluted in the Baltic States to an EU Blue Flag flyer.

Ventspils has a small Old Town, which fans out from the central **Rātslaukums** (Town Hall Square), where the attractive **Svēta Nikolaja baznīca** (St Nicholas's Church) takes centre stage. The 18th- and 19th-century buildings that line the surrounding streets are gradually being returned to their best. Amongst its most notable buildings are the **Luterāņu baznīca** (Lutheran Church) and the onion-domed **Pareiztīcīgā baznīca** (Orthodox Church).

Above: *The Livonian Order Castle in Ventspils is one of the key attractions in this increasingly vibrant port city.*

Another area that has benefited from considerable investment in recent years is the waterfront promenade **Ostas iela**, an attractive walkway adorned with various public sculptures and fountains, which borders the Old Town. From May to October river cruises also leave from here.

Ventspils also boasts a couple of decent museums. Housed in the **Livonijas ordeņa pils** (Livonian Order Castle), the **Ventspils muzejs** (Ventspils Museum) is worth visiting for that reason alone. The castle (a reasonably modest building that resembles a convent) dates back to the late 13th century, making it the oldest building in Ventspils. Inside, everything from old jewellery, weapons and books to paintings by local artists, historic photographs and an exhibition about the castle's time as a prison (1832–1959) are on display. Open daily 09:00–18:00 May–October; Tuesday–Sunday 10:00–17:00, closed Monday November–April.

Meanwhile, the **Piejuras brīvdabas muzejs** (Seaside Open-air Museum) looks at life on the Kurzeme coast, including a small section on Liv fishermen. The museum's windmill and its 1.4m (1.5yd) stretch of narrow-gauge railway, though, are the winners with children. Open daily 09:00–18:00 May–October; Tuesday–Sunday 10:00–17:00, closed Monday November to April.

Akvaparks Ventspils (Aqua Park Ventspils), with its array of swimming pools and water slides, is also popular with kids. Facilities at the adjacent sports complex include

---

BIRD HEAVEN

The large number of bird species (in excess of 250) that pass through Lake Pape National Park on their migration routes each year have helped put this reserve on the map. This is such a big deal that Lake Pape has been designated as a European IBA (Important Bird Area). To learn more about the protection of the lake and the delicate coastal ecosystem pop into the Dabas māja (Nature House) in Pape itself.

Above: *The Cathedral of St Nicholas in Liepāja is easily recognizable thanks to its striking onion-shaped domes.*

ZIEMEļVIDZEMES BIOSFĒRAS REZERVĀTS

Encompassing 60km (37 miles) of protected coastline, Ziemeļvidzemes biosfēras rezervāts (North Vidzeme Biosphere Reserve) is an important habitat for hundreds of plant species, as well as being a stop-off point for a myriad migratory birds, with the likes of crane and geese very common. Some species also choose to nest in this protected reserve. It comprises sandy beaches, expansive coastal plains and indigenous marshland.

---

tennis courts, ice-skating and a skate park. Open daily 10:00–22:00 May–September.

Liepāja ★★

Like much of Latvia, Liepāja (the country's third largest city) is still contending with the legacy of communist-era neglect. As a result, much of its Old Town is a faded echo of its former 18th- and 19th-century glory. Despite this, Liepāja still boasts a clutch of ornate wooden houses and an EU Blue Flag beach. Lying to the west of the city centre, Liepāja's main beach is backed up by the tranquil **Jūrmalas parks** (Seaside Park).

Back in the Old Town itself you can learn about the city's history at the **Vestures un mākslas muzejs** (Liepāja Museum) and take a look at **Pētera I namiņš** (Peter the Great House), where the Russian tsar laid his head when he breezed through Liepāja back in 1697. The 19th-century Lutheran **Svētā Annas baznīca** (St Anne's Church), with its impressive wooden Baroque altar, is also worth visiting, as is the striking **Svētā Jāzepa katedrāle** (Cathedral of St Joseph), the brightly coloured Orthodox **Aleksandra Nevska baznīca** (Alexander Nevsky Church) and the externally austere **Svētā Trisvienibas baznīca** (Church of the Holy Trinity), which stakes claim to housing one of the largest church organs in the world.

One of Liepāja's most intriguing areas is **Karosta**, a former Russian naval base that was closed to tourists. The fall of the Iron Curtain means that you can now visit the flamboyant Russian Orthodox **Svētā Nikolaja katedrāle** (Cathedral of St Nicholas) and tour former KGB prison cells on a 'Behind the Bars' tour.

South of Liepāja

Home to both the country's highest sand dune and its most westerly point, **Zalais Stars** (Green Ray), **Jūrmalciems** has found itself on the tourist trail. The rugged coastal scenery alone is worth stopping off for.

The leading attraction on this part of the Kurzeme coast, though, is the **Lake Pape Nature Park**, located just 10km (6 miles) from the Lithuanian border. Visitors are drawn here by the chance to see migratory birds and the reserve's increasingly famous wild horses (around 30 horses now thrive here). There is also a chance of seeing aurochs (European bison).

Vidzeme Coast

Although a popular escape with stressed city workers who flock here during summer weekends, the stretch of Vidzeme coast that strikes out north from Rīga to the Estonian border is largely overlooked by foreign visitors.

Saulkrasti

The days when **Saulkrasti** – which is actually three villages (Pabaži, Peterupe and Neibāde) joined together – was a popular spa resort may be long gone, but beaches that extend over 17km (11 miles) ensure that it remains popular with Latvians seeking a bit of summer sun. Saulkrasti also boasts two modest museums: the **Cycle Museum** and the former home of writer **Reinis Kaudzīte**.

Liepupe

An attractive settlement bisected by the River Liepupe, the eponymous village is also home to a ruined castle. Its Baltic beach, though, is the real reason to visit.

Tūja ★

On the outskirts of **Tūja** you will find the **Sarkanklints** (Red Cliffs), which take their name from the sandstone that forms them. They may be the longest of their kind in Latvia, but the seemingly endless windswept beach is the highlight.

Salacgrīva

A busy port with little to offer tourists, **Salacgrīva** is a base for boat trips to the **Randu Plavas Nature Reserve** and a **Livonian sacrificial cave** located on the Svētupe River. The administration office for the **North Vidzeme Biosphere Reserve** is also located in Salacgrīva.

Public Holidays in Latvia

1 January • **New Year's Day**
March/April • **Good Friday**
March/April • **Easter Sunday** •
March/April • **Easter Monday** •
1 May • **Labour Day**
23–24 June • **Midsummer**
11 November • **Lāčplēsis Day**
18 November • **Independence Day**
25–26 December • **Christmas Holidays**
31 December • **New Year's Eve**

Coastal Latvia at a Glance

BEST TIMES TO VISIT

June–August are the best months to visit Latvia's coast, when days tend to be hot and sunny and warm evenings mean you can make the most of alfresco dining opportunities. The shoulder months of **May** and **September** are also a good bet. Winters tend to be wetter, but days can still be clear if chilly. Pampering spa breaks tend to be cheaper out of season.

GETTING THERE

Rail: Jūrmala (Dubulti and Majori), Ventspils and Liepāja all have train stations. Direct services run to each of the cities from Rīga.
Road: In order to visit some of coastal Latvia's more remote destinations you will need a car. National bus routes include services from Rīga to Ventspils, Liepāja, Kolka and Salacgrīva.

GETTING AROUND

All of the destinations mentioned in this chapter can easily be explored on **foot**, unless you want to explore beyond the Old Towns of Ventspils and Liepāja. Travelling to and between smaller settlements like Mazirbe and Vaide, though, is only really possible if you have your own transport. **Local buses** also operate in Jūrmala, Ventspils and Liepāja. The latter has a single **tramline**.

WHERE TO STAY

LUXURY
TB Palace Hotel, Pilsonu 8, Majori, tel: 6714 7094, fax: 6714 7097, www.tbpalace.com This exclusive all-suite spa hotel offers guests an inclusive package that includes accommodation in a double suite, breakfast, a laundry service and use of the solarium and sauna, as well as transfers to and from Rīga airport. Expect to spend around € 500 for two people.
Hotel Jūrmala Spa, Jomas 47/49, Majori, Jūrmala, tel: 6778 4400, www.hotel jurmala.com This modern spa hotel boasts guest rooms that are both contemporary and comfortable. A luxurious spa with a seemingly endless list of treatments and a conference suite are also on site.
Baltic Beach Hotel, Jūras 23/25, Majori, Jūrmala, tel: 6777 1400, fax: 6777 1410, www.balticbeach.lv This five-star resort hotel reclines in an enviable beachside location and the best rooms have balconies and views of the Baltic Sea. Its spa, sea-facing restaurant and access to the Baltic Beach Sport Centre are other winning ingredients.
Amrita Hotel, Rīgas 7/9, Majori, Jūrmala, tel: 6340 3434, fax: 6348 0444, www.amrita.lv Orientated towards a business clientele, this centrally located hotel has comfortable if unremark-

able rooms, as well as its own bar and restaurant.

MID-RANGE
Alve spa Hotel, Jomas 88a, Majori, Jūrmala, tel: 6775 5970, fax: 6775 5972, www.alvespa.lv A boutique property with just 10 rooms, this is a great choice if you are looking for a cleansing retreat. Indulgent treatments offered in the spa range from thalassotherapy to body wraps.
Villa Joma, Jomas 90, Majori, Jūrmala, tel: 6777 1999, fax: 6777 1990, www. villajoma.lv This pleasant 16-room boutique hotel, housed in a traditional wooden house, has light and clean rooms. There is a restaurant on site and the beach is just minutes away.
Guest House Roze, Rožu 37, Liepāja, tel/fax: 6342 1155, www.parkhotel-roze.lv Housed in an attractively restored building adjacent to Liepāja's Seaside Park, this guesthouse boasts seven individual and contemporary rooms. The best have balconies and/or sea views.
Ostina Hotel, Dzintaru 32, Ventspils, tel: 6360 7810. Big rooms equipped with refrigerators, on-street parking and a café/restaurant help compensate for the Ostina's out-of-town location. You'll need your own wheels or a taxi to make the

Coastal Latvia at a Glance

10-minute journey across the River Venta into Ventspils.

BUDGET

Zītari, www.celotajs.lv
Rooms at Kolka's only hotel can be booked through Baltic Country Holidays. The hotel is just 500m (457yd) from Cape Kolka and all rooms are *en suite*.

Olipmskā Centra Ventspils Viesnīca, Lilas Prospekts 33, Ventspils, tel: 6362 8032, www.ocventspils.lv
Close to Ventspils's Old Town and its beach, this hotel is a real bargain. Families can cut costs even more by booking triple or quad rooms.

Peijūras Kempings Nemo, Vasarnicu 56, Ventspils, tel: 6362 7925, fax: 6362 7991, www.camping.ventspils.lv
Well located for a number of sights, such as Ventspils Seaside Open-air Museum, Seaside Park, Aqua Park and the beach. If you don't have your own camping gear then you can rent one of the wooden chalets, which sleeps four people.

Kempings Nemo, Atbalss 1, Vaivari, Jūrmala, tel: 6773 2350, fax: 6773 2349, www.nemo.lv You don't need your own tent, caravan or camper van to stay at the Nemo campground (although these are all welcome). Wooden chalets (sleeping up to eight).

Restaurant Jūrmala, (*see* Hotel Jūrmala Spa). With 280 seats this hotel restaurant probably isn't the spot for a romantic meal for two, but the stylish dining room is pleasant enough and the menu features a good range of meat and fish dishes.

Caviar Club, (*see* the Baltic Beach Hotel). Another large restaurant with a European menu; the real winners here though are the Baltic Sea views and summer terrace.

Al Thome, Pilsoņu 2, Majori, Jūrmala, tel: 6775 5755. Home-made hummus, tasty salads and melt-in-the-mouth lamb shawarma are just some of the tempting treats on the menu in this Lebanese eatery. Arabian décor and great sea views.

Sue's Asia, Jomas 74, Majori, Jūrmala, tel: 6775 5900. If you are hankering after fiery Indian, Chinese or Thai cuisine then make a beeline for Sue's Asia, another of Majori's surprisingly authentic ethnic restaurants.

Vecais Kapteinis, Dubelšteina 14, Liepāja, tel: 6342 5522. Serving up hearty Latvian cuisine in an old-world interior. Pork, ribs and potatoes come complete with lashings of sour cream. Traditionally considered to be a Christmas dish, this is also a good place to try grey peas, bacon and sour cream.

Jūrmala Tourist Information Centre, Lienes 5, Majori, Jūrmala, tel: 6714 7900, www.jurmala.lv
Ventspils Tourist Information Centre, Tirgus 7, tel: 6362 2263, www.tourism.ventspils.lv
Liepāja Tourist Information Centre, Rožu laukums 5/6, tel: 6348 0808, www.liepaja.lv
Ventspils Railway Station, Dzeizceļnieku iela.
Liepāja Railway Station, Stacijas laukums, tel: 6341 6284.
Ventspils Bus Station, Kuldīga 5.
Liepāja Bus Station, Stacijas laukums, tel: 6342 7552, www.aslap.lv

LIEPĀJA	J	F	M	A	M	J	J	A	S	O	N	D
AVERAGE TEMP. °C	-1	-2	1	5	11	14	16	16	12	8	3	0
AVERAGE TEMP. °F	29	28	34	41	52	58	62	62	55	47	39	32
RAINFALL mm	53	38	35	37	42	48	66	80	79	77	78	68
RAINFALL in	2.1	1.5	1.4	1.5	1.7	1.9	2.6	3.1	3.1	3.0	3.1	2.7
DAYS OF RAINFALL	18	16	15	14	11	15	12	12	14	15	21	19

7
Inland Latvia

Spread out over four distinctive regions – Kurzeme, Zemgale, Latgale and Vidzeme – the Latvian interior is a compelling mix of unspoiled nature offering everything from rolling hills and dense forest to vast lakes and rivers, bustling towns and sleepy villages where it often feels as if time has stood still.

The **Kurzeme** hinterland, located in the west of the country, boasts a medley of picturesque towns and villages, gushing rivers and vast swathes of forests. A region that is widely considered to be the most 'Latvian' in the country, Kurzeme is also a good place to unearth folk crafts and traditions.

South of Rīga and in the centre of Latvia, the landlocked **Zemgale** region has grown up around the Lielupe River. Amongst its attractions are urban centres like Jelgava, tracts of agricultural land and the historic palaces.

Latvia's eastern corner, **Latgale**, is a rural backwater where it often seems that the 20th, let alone the 21st, century has yet to dawn. Driving along Latgale's empty roads you are as likely to come across a horse-drawn cart or a bicycle as you are a car or a motorized tractor. Largely unspoiled by progress, bar the sprawling industrial city of Daugavpils, Latgale is an attractive region teeming with lakes and characterized by undulating hills and thick forest.

Away from the coast, **Vidzeme** is a region smothered by forest, drenched by lakes and dissected by vast rivers. A raft of crumbling castles and historical towns add to its appeal.

DON'T MISS

*** Rundāle Palace: Francesco Bartolomeo Rastrelli's 18th-century masterpiece.
*** Cēsis: one of Latvia's oldest towns boasts an abundance of old-world charm.
*** Turaida Castle: the reconstructed castle opens up stunning views over the Gauja National Park. Sculptures and gardens are amongst the complex's other attractions.
** Kuldīga: timber houses, historic churches and cobbled streets all form part of Kuldīga's allure.

Opposite: *Sigulda Castle is one of the most visited attractions in the Gauja National Park.*

KURZEME
Kuldīga **

Reclining on the banks of the Venta and Alekšupīte rivers, **Kuldīga** is one of Latvia's oldest and most attractive towns. Although Kuldīga's history can be traced back to the 13th century, its Old Town dates from the 17th and 18th centuries. A clutch of old timber houses, attractive churches, winding streets and tranquil parks combine to give Kuldīga an irresistible charm.

Consecrated in 1640, the town's oldest church, **Svētā Katrīnas baznīca** (St Catherine's Church), boasts a striking Baroque altar and sports Kuldīga's coat of arms. The **Svētā Trīsvienības baznīca** (Church of the Holy Trinity) is another Catholic house of prayer, which comes complete with an ostentatious 19th-century altar (reputedly a gift from Tsar Alexander I). Kuldīga's onion-domed **Pareizticīgā baznīca** (Orthodox Church) and the **Luteranu baznīca** (Lutheran Church) also merit a visit. Other key sights include the **Venta Bridge**, the 19th-century **Kuldīgas rajona tiesa** (Kuldīga District Court) and the mid-17th-century **Rātslaukums** (Old Town Hall Square).

To learn about Kuldīga's development pop into the **Kuldīgas muzejs** (Kuldīga Museum). The collection standouts are the old black-and-white photographs of the town. Open Tuesday–Sunday 11:00–17:00, closed Monday.

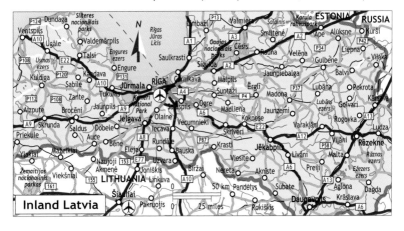

Inland Latvia

Kuldīga also stakes claim to Europe's widest waterfall, the **Ventas rumba** (Venta Waterfall). Dropping just 2m (6.5ft) it can hardly be described as a gushing cascade, but it can look pretty impressive when the river is high and water tumbles down its 250m (820ft) expanse.

Ķemeri National Park

Just west of Rīga, **Ķemeri National Park** is an oasis of dense forest and sulphurous bog. A haven for animals, birds and humans alike, Ķemeri's appeal is manifold. Wild deer and boar roam freely in some areas, while ornithologists come here to see the likes of white-tailed eagles, wood sandpipers, corncrakes, curlews and cranes (lakes **Skolas** and **Kaņieris** are popular bird-watching spots). Other visitors simply set out on one of the waymarked nature trails.

The Kempinski Group plans to open the five-star **Ķemeri Palace Hotel** in an historic old building in 2009, which should boost tourism in both the national park and nearby Jūrmala.

Talsi *

Talsi is an attractive set piece that features a pretty settlement complete with cobbled streets, a **grassy castle mound** (once a Liv stronghold) and traditional houses framed by **Talsi ezers** (Lake Talsi). North of the lake the hillside **Luterāņu baznīca** (Lutheran Church) is worth visiting for the view alone. The outlook from the castle mound is similar.

Immediately west of the lake the **Koklētas** (the *kokle* player) memorial is another notable site. Erected in 1996, this statue of the *kokle* (Latvian harp) player pays tribute to the local insurgents who battled against Latvia's post World War II Soviet occupiers.

Visitors to the **Talsu novada muzejs** (Talsu District Museum) can learn

Below: *Talsi, nestled around a pretty lake, is one of the most attractive towns in inland Latvia.*

more about Talsi's history. Set within a peaceful park the museum is also a good place for a stroll. Open Tuesday–Sunday 10:00–17:00, closed Monday.

Pedvāles Brīvdabas Mākslas Muzejs

One of Kurzeme's most esoteric attractions, the **Pedvāles brīvdabas mākslas muzejs** (Pedvāle Open-air Art Museum) is a mixture of sculpture and modern art installations scattered over 2km^2 (0.7 sq miles). Keep your eyes peeled for the creations of the park's founder, Ojārs Feldbergs, as well as some inspired and interactive pieces.

ZEMGALE
Jelgava *

The biggest city in Zemgale, **Jelgava** enjoys a dramatic natural setting, spread out on the banks of the Lielupe, Driksa and Platone rivers. Nestled on an island between the Lielupe and Driksa, **Jelgava pils** (Jelgava Palace) is the city's most attractive feature. Completed in 1772, this stunning building showcases the unmistakeable design touches of **Francesco Bartolomeo Rastrelli**, the renowned architect behind the Hermitage in St Petersburg and Jelgava Palace's more heralded sibling, the nearby Rundāle Palace.

Unfortunately for visitors the palace functions as the **Latvijas lauksaimniecības universitāte** (University of Agriculture). A small museum attempts to convey a sense of its former grandeur, yet falls somewhat short of the mark. To really see the interior you need to book onto a guided tour, which is difficult if you are not part of a group.

A handful of interesting sights dot the left bank of the Driksa and can be found by wandering down **Jāņa Čakstes Bulvāris** to **Akadēmijas iela** and the streets that branch off to the west. Heading south from Jelgava Palace brings you to the statue of **Jānis Čakste**, who became the first president of an independent Latvia in 1922. Looming behind the revered gentleman is the **Svētā Trīsvienības tornis** (Holy Trinity Tower).

Further south the **Akadēmijas Petrina un Vēstures un mākslas muzejs** (Academia Petrina and the Museum of History and Art) is housed in a charming timber-framed

---

LATVIA'S 'MOUNTAINS'

Alpine explorer types should not get too excited, but Latvia does have its uplands. The Vidzeme Uplands (or the Vidzemes Augstiene) lie east of Rīga. It is here that you will find the country's highest point, the hill of Gaziņkalns, which rises to 312m (1023ft) above sea level. The Uplands are also home to the country's small-scale ski industry and are littered with eye-catching lakes.

building. Nearby, the colourful **Svētā Simeona un Svētās Annas pareizticīgo katedrāle** (St Simeon and St Anna Orthodox Cathedral) boasts unmistakable blue domes and a lovely interior.

Rail enthusiasts should pop into the **Latvijas dzelzceļa muzeja filiāle** (Railway Museum). Close by you will also find a socialist-era throwback, the **Piemineklis Jelgavas atbrīvotājiem** (Monument to the Liberators of Jelgava), which commemorates the might of the Soviet army.

Above: *Lavish Rundāle Palace is the most striking of Latvia's grand historical palaces and was built by the same architect behind the Winter Palace in St Petersburg.*

Rundāles Pils (Rundāle Palace) ★★★

One of Latvia's iconic attractions, **Rundāles pils** (Rundāle Palace) is a grandiose 18th-century mansion whose spectacular façade is a masterpiece of Baroque and Rococo architecture. Built at the behest of Ernst Johann von Biron, the Duke of Courland, the project's success was guaranteed when **Francesco Bartolomeo Rastrelli** came on board. Although on a much smaller scale than the architect's famed Winter Palace, this opulent summer retreat bears a striking resemblance to its St Petersburg sibling.

Ongoing renovation work hopes to return the internal spaces to their original splendour. Since restoration work began in earnest back in 1972 almost a third of the palace has been sympathetically refurbished. Open daily 10:00–16:00 May, September and October; daily 10:00–19:00 June–August; daily 10:00–17:00 November–April.

Mežotnes Pils

Mežotnes pils (Mežotne Palace) is another well-known Zemgale palace whose history can be traced back to the end of the 18th century. Progress has transformed this neoclassical treasure into a five-star hotel and casual visitors are discouraged. A good time to visit is during the third weekend in July when the **Festival of Ancient Music** brings performance arts to Mežotne Palace, Rundāle Palace and Bauska Castle.

DOWDY DAUGAVPILS

You have to feel a bit sorry for old Daugavpils. It may be Latvia's second most populous city, but few tourists ever bother exploring it. It is unfortunately the archetypal Soviet-era industrial city, despite a history that does stretch back to the 13th century. Guidebook writers often try to make it sound more interesting than it is as they feel compelled to write about it. If you do feel inclined to visit then you will risk spending some precious days of your trip finding out if it merits a mention.

Bauska ★

If you're planning to visit Rundāle Palace, then it is worth stopping off in Bauska, 12km (7 miles) away. The town has a small museum, the **Bauskas novadpētniecības un mākslas muzejs** (Bauska Museum of Regional Studies), but the real reason to visit is the ruined **Bauskas Pils** (Bauska Castle). Constructed by the Livs in the 15th century, the fortification was largely destroyed around 300 years later by Peter the Great. Restoration work is ongoing and it remains an impressive site complete with sturdy walls. A reconstructed tower and some rebuilt rooms offer a glimpse into the castle's history through old clothes and other artefacts.

LATGALE
Jēkabpils

Nestled on the banks of the River Daugava, **Jēkabpils**'s Baroque centre harbours six churches, with the **Vectincībnieku baznīca** (Old Believer's Church) and the **Svētā Gara pareizticīgo** (The Church of the Holy Ghost and monastery) the cream of the crop.

For anyone with more than a passing interest in Latgale's agricultural history, **Sēlu sēta** (Selian Farmstead) is also worth popping into. Other examples of 19th-century architecture can be found on **Pastas iela**, with the houses at numbers 77, 79 and 81–87 particularly noteworthy. Meanwhile, Jēkabpils's oldest domicile is located on **Brīvības iela**.

Aglona ★

This vast white Catholic cathedral, whose two 50m (164ft) high towers dominate the landscape, is the biggest pilgrimage destination in Latvia. On various days throughout the religious calendar thousands of Catholics descend on **Aglona**, with the Feast of the Assumption (15 August) commanding crowds of around 150,000. The enchanting torch-lit procession the night before is another key time to visit.

Rēzekne

Rēzekne is a neat little town laid on a grid. There may not be enough here to keep you occupied for more than a few of hours, but it is worth visiting if you are in the vicinity.

The town's premier sight is the **Latgales māra** (Māra of Latgale), which unfortunately sits in the middle of a busy roundabout. Conceived as a celebration of freedom from Bolshevik rule back in 1920, the meaning behind the statue has now changed so that it represents a symbol of Latvian independence. After an absence of more than four decades, Māra (a Latvian goddess who champions nature and peace) was returned to her rightful place in 1992.

Rēzekne's other sights include the **Monument to the [Soviet] Liberators of Rēzekne**, a voluminous cathedral and a couple of churches.

Above: Inland Latvia, with its many lakes and forests, has plenty of accommodation on hand to offer a real escape from the hustle and bustle of the modern world.

Ludza *

Fringed by forest and lakes, **Ludza** is one of Latvia's oldest and prettiest towns. It may be in ruins, but the red-brick **Ludzas pils** (Ludza Castle) is one of country's most impressive fortifications; it also affords panoramic views out over the town to the Latgale lakes and countryside beyond.

Latgale Lakes

As the name Latgale (Land of Blue Lakes) suggests, this is a region teeming with tree-shrouded lakes. **Lubāns ezers** (Lake Lubāns), Latvia's largest lake and an important migratory bird habitat; **Rāznas ezers** (Lake Rāzna), the country's second largest lake; and **Ežezers ezers** (Lake Ežezers), a unique wetland area with 36 islands, are all popular. Latgale also boasts the deepest lake (63m/207ft at its deepest point) in the Baltic States, **Drīdzis ezers** (Lake Dridzis).

VIDZEME
Cēsis ***

Inhabited since the 13th century, **Cēsis** is an attractive settlement awash with old wooden buildings concentrated on **Rīgas iela** (Riga Street) and cobbled **Ūndens iela** (Water Street), pretty churches and the impressive ruined **Livonijas**

> ### GAUJA NATIONAL PARK
>
> Latvia's premier nature reserve, a green oasis spanning 920km² (355 sq miles) and fanning out from the River Gauja, Gaujas Nacionālā Parka (Gauja National Park) is popular with everyone from canoeists, hikers and adrenaline junkies through to picnicking families. The park also features a ruined castle and a cable car and is a favourite of Rīgans wanting to relax at weekends. For more information visit: www.gnp.lv

ordeņa Cēsu mūra pils (Cēsis Castle of the Livonian Order).

As well as this, Cēsis also boasts a 'new' castle – **Cēsu jaunā pils**, an attractive manor house containing an art and history museum that was built in the 18th century. Another historic building is the defunct 16th-century **brewery**, with production having moved out to a more modern facility outside of town.

Other sights to look out for include the **Uzvaras piemineklis** (Victory Monument), the 19th-century **Tiesa** (courthouse) and the last remaining medieval portal, the **Raunas vārti** (Rauna Gate).

Āraišu Ezerpils

Step back to the 9th century at the **Āraišu ezerpils** (Āraiši Lake Fortress), 7km (4 miles) south of Cēsis, where 15 replica log cabins cluster together on a small islet. Paddling to the islet in a dugout canoe is all part of the fun.

Sigulda *

A good place for incursions into the **Gauja National Park** (*see* panel, page 89), Sigulda is a leafy suburb whose only real sights are its old **Bruņinieks pils** (Knights Castle) and **Jaunā pils** (New Castle). The former, a rambling ruin, boasts jaw-dropping views over the Gauja Valley below; the latter an attractive 19th-century mansion. To get a bird's-eye view of the valley's dramatic scenery, take a cable car to **Krimulda pils** (Krimulda Castle).

Turaidas Pils ★★★

Located just north of Sigulda, the red-brick **Turaidas pils** (Turaida Castle) is one of Latvia's leading attractions. This is somewhat ironic when you consider the fact that it is a 1950s reconstruction, the original having been destroyed by fire in 1776 (a lightning strike ignited the castle's stock of gunpowder). While it has an obvious aesthetic appeal, the arresting views from one of three towers over the Gauja National Park are a real hit with tourists. Attractive sculptures, gentle walking trails and the 18th-century **Turaidas baznīca** (Turaida Church) also form part of the **Turaidas muzejrezervāts** (Turaida Museum Reserve).

FESTIVALS IN LATVIA

March • **Baltic Ballet Festival, Rīga** (www.ballet-festival.lv)
June • **Opera Festival, Rīga** (www.opera.lv)
July • **Sigulda Opera Festival**
August • **Liepāja Dzintars** Rock festival (www.liepajasdzintars.lv)
September • **International Chamber Music Festival, Rīga**
October • **Arēna New Music Festival, Rīga** (www.arenafest.lv)

Inland Latvia at a Glance

For hot sunny days and warm evenings **summer** is the best time to explore inland Latvia.

Rail: Direct services run from Rīga to Jelgava, Sigulda, Cēsis, Rēzekne and Ludza.
Road: Talsi, Jelgava, Kuldīga, Bauska, Sigulda, Cēsis, Aglona, Rēzekne and Ludza all have bus stations.

Buses connect towns and cities throughout inland Latvia. It is easy to get around on **foot**, by **local bus** or by **taxi**.

Mežotne Palace, Mežotnes pils, tel. 6396 0711, fax: 6396 0725, www.mezotnes pils.lv Elegant and classical guest rooms.
Dikļi Palace Hotel, Dikļi, tel: 6420 7480, fax: 620 7485, www.diklupils.lv Sleep like royalty in rooms and suites with period furniture.
Hotel Kolonna Cēsis, Vienības laukums 1, tel: 6412 0122, fax: 6412 0121, www.hotelkolonna.com Spacious rooms in the heart of the Old Town.
Hotel Kolonna Kuldīga, Pilsētas laukums 6, Kuldīga, tel: 6332 2430, fax: 6332 3671, www.hotelkolonna. com Small new town hotel housed in a 1970s building.
Hotel Kolonna Rēzekne, Brīvības 2, Rēzekne, tel: 6460

7820, fax: 6460 7825, www.hotelkolonna.com Attractive hotel on the banks of the River Rēzekne.
Hotel Sigulda, Pils 6, Sigulda, tel/fax: 6797 2263, www. hotelsigulda.lv With good quality rooms, sauna, swimming pool and a restaurant.
Talsi Hotel, Kareivju 16, Talsi, tel: 6323 2020, fax: 6323 2023, www.hoteltalsi.lv Good value rooms.
Zemgale Hotel, Rīgas 11, Jelgava, tel: 6300 7707, fax: 6300 7710, www.zemgale. info Modern and comfortable hotel. Adjacent bowling alley.
Ventas Rumba, Stendes (Martinš Island), Kuldīga, tel: 6332 4168, www.ventas rumba.lv Simple two- and four-bedded rooms.
Lauku Ceļotājs (Baltic Country Holidays), Kuģu 11, Rīga, tel: 6761 7600, fax: 6783 0041, www.celotajs.lv Accommodation agency.

Pilsmuiža, Pils 16, Sigulda, tel: 6797 4032. Providing solid Latvian food and great views of Sigulda's Old Castle.
Dikļi Palace Hotel, (see Dikļi Palace Hotel). The chef

tempts diners with local game, meat and fish dishes.
Rozalija, (see Hotel Kolonna Rēzekne). Hearty Latvian fare in pleasant surroundings.
Café Popular, (see Hotel Kolonna Cēsis). Tasty lunch and dinner menus feature tender grilled meats and fresh fish.

Kuldīga, Baznīcas 5, tel: 6332 2259, www.visitkuldiga.lv
Talsi, Liēla 19-21, tel: 6322 4165, www.talsi.lv
Jelgava, Pasta 37, tel: 6302 2751, www.jelgava.lv
Bauska, Rātslaukums 1, tel: 6392 3797, www.tourism.bauska.lv
Jēkabpils, Brīvības 140/142, tel: 6523 3822, www.jekabpils.lv
Rēzekne, Atbrīvošanas Aleja 98, tel: 6460 5505, www.rezekne.lv
Ludza, Baznīca 42, tel: 6570 7203, www.ludza.lv
Cēsis, Pils laukums 1, tel: 6412 1815, fax: 6410 7777, www.tourism.cesis.lv
Sigulda, Valdemara 1a, tel: 6797 1335, www.tourism.sigulda.lv

DAUGAVPILS	J	F	M	A	M	J	J	A	S	O	N	D
AVERAGE TEMP. °C	-5	-5	0	5	12	15	16	16	11	6	1	-3
AVERAGE TEMP. °F	-5	-5	0	5	12	15	16	16	11	6	1	-3
RAINFALL mm	37	28	32	42	52	74	79	74	69	52	51	43
RAINFALL in	1.5	1.1	1.3	1.7	2.0	2.9	3.1	2.9	2.7	2.0	2.0	1.7
DAYS OF RAINFALL	21	17	15	13	11	13	14	12	15	15	20	23

8
Tallinn

Tallinn boasts what is quite simply one of Europe's most stunning old towns, a **chocolate box pretty** historic core that most cities would kill for. Vaulting church spires, the unmistakable onion domes of its Orthodox cathedral, ancient fortifications and a collage of **Baroque** and **Medieval** buildings unite to form a postcard-perfect picture.

One of the best ways to get a feel for Tallinn is by simply meandering around its **cobbled Old Town streets**, sifting through the layers of history and taking time to appreciate the stunning architecture that greets every step. Those who want to get in and about the city are also catered for by museums, cultural venues and Tallinn's wealth of bustling cafés, bars and nightclubs.

Perhaps unsurprisingly, the Estonian capital has been earning positive comparisons to Prague. Though to simply compare this **UNESCO World Heritage** listed gem to the Czech capital does not complete the picture. Nestled in the northeastern extremity of Europe, the city enjoys an attractive and strategic location on the shores of the **Baltic Sea**. Less discovered than its Czech neighbour, Tallinn is still a city very much lived in and enjoyed by the locals.

Since breaking free from the shackles of Soviet rule in 1991 Tallinn has more than made up for five decades of communist-era deprivations, effortlessly adapting to democracy and embracing capitalism. The city's inhabitants have also embraced new technologies, which is great for tourist visitors who never have to look too hard to find an Internet terminal or Wi-Fi hotspot.

DON'T MISS

*** Town Hall Square: this cobbled expanse is the epicentre of Tallinn life.
*** Medieval Fortifications: the sturdy, defensive towers and walls that surround the Old Town are impressive both in their scope and appearance.
*** Toompea: climb Toompea Hill to take in the Orthodox Cathedral, admire the castle and the centre of Estonian power, or to soak up the mesmerizing views.

Opposite: *The Alexander Nevsky Cathedral in Tallinn casts an unmistakable presence on the city skyline on Toompea Hill.*

Above: *Tallinn's Old Town Hall Square has for centuries been the hub of city life, with plenty of cafés on hand to enjoy a spot of people-watching these days.*

OLD TOWN

The UNESCO World Heritage Site that is Tallinn's **Vanalinn** (Old Town) is effectively the city's main attraction; a compact oasis crammed with historic architecture and fringed by the hulking remains of sturdy medieval walls and fortified towers.

Raekoja Plats ★★★

Raekoja plats (Town Hall Square), the expansive square at the nucleus of the Old Town, is the place to come and watch local life bustle past from the comfort of a pavement café, or to seek refuge from the bracing winter air. The attractive cobbled plaza has been integral to city life for centuries, serving as a place for public executions, mass celebration and a market place over the years.

The centrepiece of the square is the late Gothic **Tallinna raekoda** (Tallinn Town Hall) whose sturdy spire stretches for the sky and hangs high above the piazza. A civic building has stood on this spot since the 14th century, although most of the present structure dates from the early 15th century. The second floor tends to be used exclusively for private functions; however, the general public can visit the exhibition hall located in the three-nave cellar. Open Tuesday–Saturday 10:00–16:00, closed Sunday and Monday mid-May to mid-October; closed late October to early May.

A visit to the **Raeapteek** (Town Hall Pharmacy), which is also located on the square, takes you back to the early 15th century and one of the oldest operational pharmacies in Europe. The medicines dispensed may be modern, but the interior has been kept as original as possible. One medicinal relic that tourists are welcome to try is the spiced claret that was thought to aid digestion and be a cure for a variety of ailments, including the plague. Open daily 10:00–18:00.

Medieval Fortifications ***

At the extremities of the Old Town you will come across a collection of literally unmissable fortifications. The thick walls and towers that encircled Vanalinn in the late 13th and early 14th century were gradually expanded upon, and by the 16th century the Estonian capital boasted a defence system that was the envy of many of its Northern European neighbours. Back then the sturdy town wall was 3m (10ft) thick, stood 16m (52ft) high and stretched 4km (2.5 miles) around the city. It also boasted a phenomenal 46 defence towers. Just over half of this (2km/1.2 miles of wall and 26 towers) still stands today. Most of the towers are inaccessible to the public, with the exception of the neighbouring **Nana**, **Sauna** and **Kuldjala Towers**. Open Tuesday–Friday 13:00–18:00, Saturday 10:00–14:00, closed Sunday and Monday.

Situated on Toompea Hill (see page 98), **Kiek in de kök** (Peek in the Kitchen) is an imposing 15th-century cannon tower. Upon completion the tower boasted 4m (13ft) thick walls and had a diameter of 17m (56ft) and stood 38m (125ft) tall. Its unusual name comes from the fact that the tower guard had a clear view into neighbouring kitchens.

Today the tower, which has been reconstructed at various intervals, documents the city's military history. In 2007 some of the secret tunnels under the city walls were reopened. Admission is by guided tour only (tel: 644 6686) with groups meeting here. Open Tuesday–Sunday 10:30–17:00, closed Monday November–February; Tuesday–Sunday 10:30–18:00, closed Monday March–October.

In the north the **Suur rannavärav** (Great Coastal Gate) and **Paks Margareeta** (Fat Margaret's Tower) were constructed to protect Vanalinn against attack from the sea. Today the defunct fortification houses the **Eesti meremuuseum** (Estonian Maritime Museum), which is worth visiting if only for the elevated views over the bay and back to the Old Town. Open Wednesday–Sunday 10:00–18:00, closed Monday and Tuesday.

Two of Tallinn's other ancient portals, the **Viru väravad** (Viru Gates), delineate the eastern entrance to the Old Town.

ESTONIAN FLAG

The Estonian tricolour is a striking flag made up of equal horizontal segments of blue, black and white from top to bottom respectively. Interestingly, it first emerged as a student flag in Tartu in the 1880s before being hoisted as the flag of the independent nation in 1918. It fluttered above Tallinn and around the country until the Russians swept through in 1940 and it did not return until independence.

BREAKING AWAY

Despite the fact that many Estonians have lived much of their life under Soviet rule and can speak Russian, few these days are keen to admit it let alone talk about it. A certain amount of understandable revisionism has swept through the country with all images of Russian leaders dislodged and the Russian language being vanquished from all signs and abandoned in schools. In recent years there have been grumblings from some older people that some aspects of life were better in Soviet times, but few genuinely hanker after a return to the communist days.

Tallinna Linnamuuseum ★★

Anyone who wants to learn more about Tallinn's fascinating history should make a beeline for **Tallinna linnamuuseum** (Tallinn City Museum). Here you can trace the city's evolution from medieval times though to its 1991 independence. Open Wednesday–Monday 10:30–17:00, closed Tuesday November–February; Wednesday–Monday 10:30–18:00, closed Tuesday March–October.

Suurgildi Hoone ★

The **Suurgildi hoone** (Great Guild Hall), the former meeting place of Tallinn's wealthy merchants, dates from 1417. This grand building, beaten only by the town hall (excluding religious buildings) when it came to size in the medieval city, was constructed as an ostentatious display of affluence and power. Both the exterior (look out for the Great Guild's coat of arms) and interior largely retain their original appearance. Home to the **Eesti ajaloomuuseum** (Estonian History Museum), the hall is open to the public. Open Thursday–Tuesday 11:00–18:00, closed Wednesday.

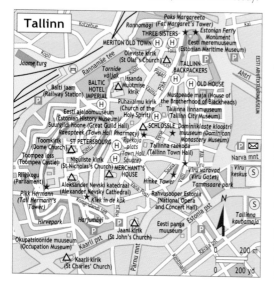

Mustpeade Maja ★★

Another guild house worth seeking out is the **Mustpeade maja** (House of the Brotherhood of Blackheads). This is one of the few Renaissance buildings still standing in Tallinn. Membership to the Brotherhood of the Blackheads (an organization that dates from 1399) was seen as a stepping stone to joining the Great Guild. Unlike its bigger sibling, this mercantile club also accepted foreign members. The exterior of the property, which features intricate carvings, dates from the 16th century and the colourful door from 1640. The neoclassical interior is the result of a 1908 makeover.

Oleviste Kirik

When the church was consecrated in the late 13th century the 140m (259ft) steeple protruding towards heaven rendered **Oleviste kirik** (St Olaf's Church) the tallest building in Europe. According to the city authorities it was the world's tallest building in 1500, when it stood 159m (522ft) tall.

Today, the tower (a 19th-century replacement) stretches up a mere 120m (394ft) and is a minnow when it comes to world architecture. This attractive church is still a main feature of the city's skyline. Open during church services.

Niguliste Kirik

Heralded as one of the best examples of a medieval church in Estonia, **Niguliste kirik** (St Nicholas's Church) was constructed in the early 13th century (although much of what you see today is the result of 15th- and 20th-century reconstructions). It pre-dates the Old Town's sturdy fortifications, and it is believed that the church originally undertook both an ecclesiastical and a defensive role.

The artistic treasures displayed inside the church mean that it has been designated as a museum. Intricate carvings, ornate chandeliers, the late 15th-century high altar, the 16th-century altar of St Anthony and an early section of Berndt Notke's *Danse Macabre* are among its treasures. Open Wednesday–Sunday 10:00–17:00, closed Monday and Tuesday.

Pühavaimu Kirik

The humble 14th-century **Pühavaimu kirik** (Church of the Holy Spirit) is important for a number of reasons. Firstly it is the oldest religious building in Tallinn dating from this period. Perhaps more important was the role that it played in the promotion of the Estonian language, with services held in the native tongue and former pastor, Johann Knoell, credited as the author of the first book published in Estonian, *Catechism*, in 1535. In addition, the late 15th-century altar,

A MIGHTY BELL

Not only does Tallinn's Aleksander Nevski katedraal (Alexander Nevsky Cathedral) strike an unmistakable presence on the city skyline, but it also boasts the Estonian capital's largest cupola and also the city's most enormous bell. Weighing in at 15,000kg (15 tonnes), the bell is one of 11 that ring out as a reminder that a service is imminent. Services take place daily at 08:30 and 17:00.

the work of Berndt Notke, is considered one of the most valuable pieces of medieval sculpture in the country. Open Monday–Saturday 09:30–17:30, Sunday 10:00–16:00 January–April; Monday–Saturday 09:30–18:30, Sun 10:00–18:30 May–August. Daily 10:00–17:30 September–December.

Dominiiklaste Kloostri Muuseum

Dating from 1246, St Catherine's Monastery is the oldest preserved building in Tallinn's Old Town. More than just a place of worship, the monastery has also functioned as a school. Today it is home to the **Dominiiklaste kloostri muuseum** (Dominican Monastery Museum) and is worth visiting to admire its Gothic appearance, to learn more about the Dominicans in Tallinn and to see its ornate cloisters and extensive collection of carved stones. Open daily 10:00–18:00 mid-May to late September. By appointment late September to mid-May.

Toompea ★★★

The short but steep ascent up Toompea Hill more than rewards the effort. Highlights up here include **Toompea loss** (Toompea Castle) and the **Aleksander Nevski katedraal** (Alexander Nevsky Cathedral), the **Riigikogu** (Estonian Parliament) and **Pikk Hermann** (Tall Hermann's Tower), which proudly flies the Estonian flag.

Below: *The view of Tallinn and its rambling spires from Toompea Hill is worth the hike up from the Old Town.*

Dating from 1900, the Orthodox cathedral, constructed at the behest of Tsar Alexander III, boasts striking black onion domes and is the most attractive place of worship in the city. Much younger than its neighbouring churches, it has apparently suffered from a number of structural problems, which locals claim is due to the fact that it was built in honour of a Russian hero, but is, somewhat erroneously, located on the grave of an Estonian one. Open daily 08:00–19:00.

Most visitors climb Toompea, however, for the sweeping views back across Tallinn and out to the Baltic Sea. This dramatic vista can best be appreciated from one of two viewing platforms.

Toompea Street is also home to the **Okupatsioonide muuseum** (Occupation Museum). Sobering artefacts hark back to the bleak periods of both Soviet and Nazi occupation. Open Tuesday–Sunday 11:00–18:00, closed Monday.

BEYOND THE OLD TOWN
Estonian Ferry Monument

To the north of the Old Town on the way to Tallinn's port, the **Estonian Ferry Monument** may not be one of Tallinn's most flamboyant sights, but it is one of its most poignant: a reminder of the 1994 ferry disaster. On 28 September the Stockholm-bound *MS Estonia* sank in the pitch dark Baltic Sea, plunging 852 passengers and crew to their deaths.

Eesti Arhitektuurimuuseum

To learn more about Tallinn's rich architectural heritage, or to see temporary exhibitions dedicated to triumphs and tragedies in building design from around the globe, then head to the **Eesti arhitektuurimuuseum** (The Museum of Estonian Architecture), which is housed in Rottermann's Salt Storage House down near the harbour. Open Wednesday–Friday 12:00–20:00, Saturday and Sunday 11:00–18:00, closed Monday and Tuesday in summer; Wednesday to Sunday 11:00–18:00, closed Monday and Tuesday in winter.

FURTHER AFIELD
Kadrioru Loss **

A handful of attractions are clustered in Tallinn's northeastern suburbs. Of these, **Kadrioru loss** (Kadriorg Palace), commissioned by Peter the Great in 1718 in an extravagant display of affection for his wife Catherine, is the most impressive. The graceful Baroque building also houses the **Kadrioru kunstimuuseum** (Kadriorg Art Museum). One of five locations where the **Eesti kunstimuuseum** (Art Museum of Estonia) exhibits its collection, Kadriorg contains paintings crafted mainly by foreign artists. The palace is worth visiting

PIRITA

The one-time location of the 1980 Moscow Olympics, Pirita (around a 15-minute car ride from the centre of Tallinn) is renowned locally for its sandy beach. Much of Pirita's infrastructure was purpose-built for the Olympic sailing events, including the marina, coastal highway and TV tower. This booming residential district is also home to the eponymous River Pirita, a 15th-century convent and thick forest.

just for the chance to stroll around its elegant grounds. Open Tuesday–Sunday 10:00–17:00, closed Monday May–September; Wednesday–Sunday 10:00–17:00, closed Monday October–April.

Mikkeli Muuseum

The private collection of Johannes Mikkel is in an adjacent building, the **Mikkel Museum**. It may not be worth making the trip out of town for alone, but the gallery does have a decent collection of Dutch and Flemish paintings as well as artefacts from around the globe. Open Wednesday–Sunday 11:00–17:00, closed Monday and Tuesday.

Eduard Vilde Muuseum

Nearby, the **Eduard Vilde muuseum** (Eduard Vilde Museum) commemorates the life and writing of the renowned Estonian author. For non-Estonians the exhibition of contemporary art on display in the **Kastellaani galerii** (Kastellaani Gallery) may be of more interest. Open Wednesday–Monday 11:00–17:00, closed Tuesday January, February, November and December; Wednesday–Monday 11:00–18:00, closed Tuesday March–October.

Tammsaare Muuseum

The life and work of another famous Estonian literary figure, Anton Hansen Tammsaare, is commemorated just off the main Narva Mnt road in the **Tammsaare muuseum** (Tammsaare Museum). Tammsaare's seminal work, *Truth and Justice*, earned him the reputation as the country's best 20th-century author.

Eesti Ajaloomuuseum ★★

Heading further east along the coast brings you to **Maarjamäe loss** (Maarjamäe Palace) and the **Eesti ajaloomuuseum** (Estonian History Museum), which documents the country's long and difficult path to self-government. Open Wednesday–Sunday 11:00–18:00, closed Monday and Tuesday March to October; Wednesday–Sunday 10:00–17:00, closed Monday and Tuesday November to February.

Soviet Tallinn
Tallinna Teletorn *
It may be a bit of an eyesore, but the concrete monstrosity that is the **Tallinna teletorn** (Tallinn TV Tower) has a number of redeeming features. First and foremost are the far-reaching views afforded by the 170m (558ft) viewing platform. On a good day these stretch out across the Baltic Sea and back to the Old Town. Open daily 10:00–24:00.

Former KGB Headquarters
Home to the present-day Interior Ministry, the former KGB Headquarters at Pikk 61 are not an official tourist sight. This building with bricked-up cellar windows is interesting, nonetheless, as the place where misery was inflicted upon the countless dissidents facing deportation to Siberia. The cellar housed the cells where the deportees were incarcerated prior to their journey. During Soviet times people apparently joked that this must be the tallest building on the globe because it was possible to see Siberia from the basement.

Maarjamäe War Memorial
The overblown obelisk situated on the Pirita Highway forms part of the larger Maarjamäe War Memorial complex, whose imposing concrete sculptures were typical of the 1950s and 60s; dedicated to Soviet heroism they are marked by triumphalist gestures. The vaulting spire commemorates the loss of Russian lives during World War I, while the iron and concrete statues commemorate Soviet bravery during World War II.

The Bronze Soldier
A rare relic of communism, the **Bronze Soldier**, which was controversially located outside the National Library for 50 years, is another tribute to the bravery of Russian troops during World War II. Many locals saw it as a celebration of the postwar Soviet occupation of Estonia and repeatedly called for its removal. In April 2007 the government finally ordered its relocation to Tallinn's military cemetery.

Below: *The controversial Bronze Soldier monument that sparked riots amongst the city's Russian population in 2007.*

Tallinn at a Glance

BEST TIMES TO VISIT

May–September are the best months to visit. From late spring until early autumn days are warm and the city's colourful bars and cafés spill out onto the Old Town streets. In the shoulder seasons temperatures cool considerably after dark, so you will need some warm clothing. Winters can be very cold and wet.

GETTING THERE

Rail: Domestic train services link Tallinn to Tartu, Valga, Türi, Viljandi, Tapa, Narva and Pärnu.
Road: The main bus routes into Tallinn come from Tartu, Pärnu, Viljandi, Rakvere, Narva, Kuressaare and Haapsalu.

GETTING AROUND

The good news is that most of Tallinn's historic Old Town is pedestrianized. Its reasonably compact size means that most visitors can easily explore the historic core on **foot**. City **buses**, **trolleybuses**, **trams** and **taxis** also operate. Bus, trolleybus and tram tickets can be bought at news kiosks and from the driver.

WHERE TO STAY

LUXURY
Schlossle, Pühavaimu 13/15, tel: 699 7700, fax: 699 7777, www.schlossle-hotels.com When it comes to old-world luxury the boutique Schlossle is hard to beat. Tallinn's old-

est five-star hotel has long been impressing guests with its attentive service and first-class location.
St Petersbourg, Rataskaevu 7, tel: 628 6500, fax: 628 6565, www.schlossle-hotels.com More affordable than its illustrious sibling, the Schlossle, this central hotel offers comfortable and luxurious rooms. It can be a bit noisy at times with noise from the street and, on our visit, the sauna located immediately above our room.
Radisson SAS, Rävala 3, tel: 682 3000, fax: 382 3001, www.radissonsas.com Sacrificing an Old Town location is rewarded by large and luxurious guest rooms. Other facilities at the hotel include a sauna, gym and free Internet access. Upper-floor rooms with views over the Old Town are the best. If you don't have a room with a view head to the 24th floor bar, Lounge 24.
Three Sisters, Pikk 71/Trolli 2, tel: 630 6300, fax: 630 6301, www.threesistershotel.com Check into this five-star design hotel and find yourself a part of Tallinn's history, literally. Located within the 16th-century walls the hotel also boasts a fine-dining restaurant and a wine bar.

MID-RANGE
Merchant's House Hotel, Dunkri 4, tel: 697 7500, fax: 697 7501, www. merchantshousehotel.com Straddling two 14th- and 16th-

century properties, this hotel impresses guests with neat original touches like wooden beams and restored fireplaces. Rooms are modern and comfortable and a range of massages (including a chocolate one) is also on offer.
City Hotel Portus, Uus-Sadama 23, tel: 680 6600, fax: 680 6601, www.portus.ee A combination of reasonable prices and a great location make the Portus hard to beat. The rooms are not elaborate, but many have great views and all come with air-conditioning, satellite TV and Wi-Fi.
Imperial, Nunne 14, tel: 627 4800, fax: 627 4801, www.imperial.ee Situated at the foot of Toompea Hill, the Imperial with its 32 contemporary rooms and suites, sauna, hot tub and free Internet access is another good bet.
Reval Inn, Sadama 1, tel: 667 8700, fax: 667 8800, www.revalinn.com Providing comparatively basic but comfortable and affordable accommodation just five minutes' walk from the Old Town, the 163-room Reval Inn also has a café, complimentary Internet terminals and Wi-Fi access.

BUDGET
Dzingel, Männiku tee 89, tel: 610 5201, fax: 610 5245, www.dzingel.ee With bed and breakfast for two people costing around €50 a night, free on-site parking and complimentary use of the sauna,

this hotel is a popular budget option. The only drawback is its location 6km (4 miles) from the Old Town.

Meriton Old Town, Lai 49, tel: 614 1300, fax: 614 1311, www.meritonhotels.com Near Tallinn Port this characterful hotel boasts 41 *en-suite* rooms. Great Internet rates.

Tallinn Backpackers, Lai 10, tel: 644 0298, www.tallinn backpackers.com Bag a bed in one of the 16-, 10- or six-bed dorms (the bigger the dorm the cheaper the price) at this friendly central hostel. They also have singles, doubles and triples available on nearby Viru.

Old House, Uus 22, tel: 641 1464, fax: 641 1604, www.oldhouse.ee Providing accommodation in dormitories, single, twin and quad rooms at its guesthouse and hostel, as well as private accommodation, the Old House should have something to suit your wallet.

WHERE TO EAT

Stenhus (*see* Schlossle Hotel). Feast on mouth-watering Estonian and international dishes at what is arguably the best restaurant in the Baltic States. Atmospheric surrounds and first-rate service make the hefty price tag worthwhile.

Egoist, Vene 33, tel: 646 4052. If you want to dine in this perennially popular restaurant you'll need to book well in advance. Fabulous

cooking and a great wine list are the main components of Egoist's winning formula.

Silk, Kullasepa 4, tel: 648 4625. Popular with the city's beautiful people, this stylish sushi restaurant is the place to be seen. The food is excellent.

Olde Hansa, Vana turg 1, tel: 627 9020. Enjoy a slice of medieval Tallinn at this restaurant, where staff don the costumes of a bygone era and litres of hoppy beer help the hearty meat dishes on their way.

Pegasus, Harju 1, tel: 631 4040. Drink with the in-crowd in the ground floor bar or make your way upstairs to enjoy sumptuous and innovative world cuisine.

SHOPPING

Alongside the tourist orientated souvenir and craft shops Tallinn's **Old Town** also boasts a clutch of fashion boutiques (including big names like Hugo Boss, Maxmara and Tango) and off-licences selling the local potent alcoholic tipple **Vana Tallinn**. The quality and type of traditional keepsakes on

sale vary considerably, but include ceramic models of Old Town buildings, hand-knitted garments, wooden handicrafts and amber imported from Latvia and Lithuania. For a more hard-core retail experience you might want to head to one of Estonia's out-of-town malls. Tallin's street markets are also well worth investigating.

TOURS AND EXCURSIONS

Bus tours: Hop-on hop-off city tours follow three routes: the red, blue and green line. The latter has the most stops and runs out to Kadriorg. **Walking tours:** Pick up an audio guide (www.audio guide.ee) or book a guided tour at the Tourist Office.

USEFUL CONTACTS

Tourist Information Centre, Niguliste 2, tel: 645 7777, www.tourism.tallinn.ee **Railway Station**, Toompuiestee 37, tel: 1444 or (372) 615 6851, www.baltijaam.ee **Bus Station**, Lastekodu 46, tel: 12550, www.bussiriside.ee **Hop-on Hop-off City Tours**, www.citytour.ee

TALLINN	J	F	M	A	M	J	J	A	S	O	N	D
AVERAGE TEMP. °C	-3	-5	-1	3	10	13	16	15	10	6	1	-2
AVERAGE TEMP. °F	25	23	30	39	50	57	62	60	51	43	34	28
RAINFALL mm	48	32	32	37	38	57	78	52	74	73	67	57
RAINFALL in	1.9	1.3	1.3	1.5	1.5	2.2	3.1	2.0	2.9	2.9	2.6	2.2
DAYS OF RAINFALL	11	8	8	7	7	8	11	11	12	11	14	14

9
Coastal Estonia

Estonia boasts a shoreline that belies its size, with 1242km (772 miles) of coast on the mainland and 2552km (1586 miles) fringing over 1500 islands. With a total of **3794km** (2358miles) of indented seashore, you won't have to look too far, even in the height of the summer season, to find your own sheltered stretch of coastline.

The majority of the country's isles and islets are uninhabited, and a substantial number are protected nature reserves (around 20% of the coast is protected in some form). This means that tourism is largely concentrated on the largest of Estonia's islands: **Saaremaa** and **Hiiumaa**. Even on these islands development remains pleasantly low-key. In addition to unspoiled rural scenery and rich cultural traditions (preserved, at least in part, by their relative isolation during Estonia's absorption into the USSR), the country's populated islands also boast ancient settlements complete with medieval fortifications and imposing churches.

White sand beaches at **Pärnu** and **Haapsalu** ensure the popularity of both towns with domestic and, increasingly, foreign visitors. The latter is blessed with an impressive 13th-century castle, while Pärnu is also a well-established spa resort (thanks to the local mineral-rich mud). Investment in hotels and wellness facilities means that **Kuressaare**, the main town on Saaremaa, is also giving Pärnu a run for its money in the rest-and-relaxation stakes.

Estonians are justifiably proud of their beautiful coastline and the growth in tourism to this region is being implemented with sustainability and conservation in mind.

DON'T MISS

*** Lahemaa National Park: showcasing the best of Estonia's northern coastline, a mystical landscape of sandy dunes, erratic boulders and traditional wooden houses.
*** Pärnu: this is Estonia's top coastal resort.
*** Saaremaa: offers everything from unspoiled nature to striking historic monuments.
** Haapsalu: home to one of Estonia's dramatic castles.
** Paldiski: a fascinating throwback to the country's Soviet era.

Opposite: *Bishop's Castle, Kuressaare, is a medieval episcopal castle.*

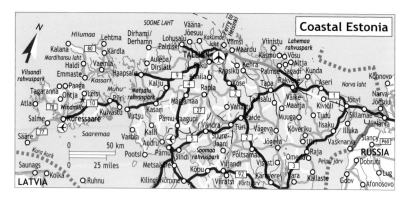

NORTH COAST

Estonia's windswept north coast is distinguishable from that in the west by the presence of dramatic limestone cliffs. This part of Estonia is punctuated with deserted naval bases, striking fortresses and charming lighthouses, as well as the rugged beauty of the Lahemaa National Park.

Paldiski **

A former Soviet naval base, **Paldiski**, located 45km (30 miles) west of Tallinn, was once one of the busiest ports in the Russian Empire. Established by **Peter the Great** in 1718, it became a Soviet naval base in 1939 and, later, a training ground for the crew of the USSR's nuclear submarines.

Abandoned by the Soviets in 1994, a collection of run-down and derelict buildings provide an insight into the military might that propped up the old Iron Curtain (at one time more than 16,000 military personnel were based here). Things to look out for include woeful vacant apartment blocks, the (never completed) five-pointed **Peetri kindlus** (Peter's Fortress) and Estonia's tallest lighthouse, **Pakri majakas** (Pakri Lighthouse), which is 52m (171ft) high. A couple of semi-restored churches, two naval graveyards, the 19th-century railway station and Paldiski's old submarine training base are also worth visiting. Investment in the area means that eventually these forceful reminders may, like the Soviet navy itself, disappear.

CLIMATE

Its northerly locale means that the Estonian coast has a slightly harsher climate than that of Latvia and Lithuania further to the south. This said, long summer days benefit from eight or nine hours of sunshine, with daytime highs reaching the early to mid-20s. Winters tend to be harsh with the average temperature plummeting as low as -7°C (19°F) in January and February. August is the wettest month, with February the driest.

Viimsi

Traditionally a place where city dwellers had their weekend and summer homes, the **Viimsi Peninsula**, 20km (12 miles) to the east of Tallinn, is a booming residential suburb. The small cape is also home to a number of hotels. A smattering of lighthouses and the **Kindral Laidoneri muuseum** (General Laidoner Museum) aside, Viimsi has few sights as such.

The latter carries the dual title of the **Estonian War Museum** (Eesti sõjamuuseum) and commemorates both the life of the celebrated military leader Johan Laidoner and the role of the country's army throughout history.

Lahemaa Rahvuspark ★★★

Heading northeast from Tallinn brings you to what is arguably the premier attraction on the country's northern shoreline, **Lahemaa rahvuspark** (Lahemaa National Park). Established in 1971 and spanning an area of 725km^2 (280 sq miles) – 474 km^2 (183 sq miles) on land and 251km^2 (97 sq miles) of sea – Lahemaa has the honour of being both the largest and the oldest national park in Estonia.

Situated about 80km (50 miles) from the capital, this conservation area boasts ancient woodlands, peaty bogs and a coastline dotted with erratic boulders.

The relaxed pace of life and the 'getting-away-from-it-all' feeling are Lahemaa's main drawcards. This also means, however, that facilities and public transport are rather limited, so you'll need a hire car to explore (better still, ditch motorized transport and rent a bicycle instead).

Seemingly innocuous, **Viinistu**, located at the northeastern tip of the Pärispea Peninsula, is home to one of Estonia's best art museums. The eponymous **Viinistu kunstimuuseum** (Viinistu Art Museum) houses a permanent collection of 20th-century Estonian art, as well as hosting various temporary exhibitions. For visitors one of the most striking exhibits are the 100 concrete suitcases that sit outside the museum, paying their silent respects to those banished by the Red Army.

Käsmu has an important shipbuilding heritage and a visit to the slightly eccentric **meremuuseum** (Maritime Museum) is worthwhile. Curator and owner Aarne Vaik spent more than two decades collecting the nautical

PAKRI PENINSULA

In sharp contrast to the ghostly Paldiski naval base, the Pakri Peninsula, on which Paldiski is situated, is an impressive natural sight boasting dramatic limestone cliffs and a nesting ground for various bird species. This contrast between re-flowering nature and the rotting remains of the once mighty Soviet Union is a telling microcosm for the whole of the Baltic region.

FAUNA AND FLORA OF LAHEMAA NATIONAL PARK

This bountiful national park lies on the coast to the east of the capital and is well worth visiting for its breadth of flora and fauna. It boasts more than 800 species of plant life and over 50 mammal residents. Then there are the birds, over 200 species of which migrate through annually with many of these choosing to nest here too. In autumn locals flock here to pick mushrooms, though be very careful if you follow suit, as some are poisonous.

memorabilia that is on display. There is little else to do in the village, bar take a bracing stroll on a remote and deserted beach or pick up a forest trail.

Võsu, 8km (5 miles) to the east, is popular with holidaying Estonians primarily because of its sandy beach, which has been awarded a Blue Flag by the EU.

Once a prosperous fishing village, **Altja**, 18km (11 miles) further on, is worth visiting to see its collection of renovated wooden buildings and to dine in its 19th-century inn.

Heading slightly inland, the architectural highlight of the park is the 19th-century **Palmse mõis** (Palmse Manor), which is heralded as one of the most attractive Baltic-German estates in the Baltic region. In addition to tours of the mansion, Palmse boasts woodland walks, a swan lake and an exhibition of old motor vechicles. **The Lahemaa National Park Visitor Centre** is also located within the manor, and there is a café, hotel and restaurant on site.

Lahemaa's other stately home, **Sagadi mõis** (Sagadi Manor), was constructed in 1749. Like Palmse it is open to the public and has pleasant grounds. For anyone who wants to learn about Estonia's forests it also has a **forestry museum**.

Below: Haapsalu Episcopal Castle is a well-preserved castle complex on the coast that is steeped in history and legend.

Narva *

Geographically closer to St Petersburg than to Tallinn, **Narva** is the third largest city in Estonia. Its population is also around 90% Russian, making it distinctly different to anywhere else in the country. Demarcating east from west, Narva's key sight is an imposing 14th-century castle,

which has challenged the Russian castle in Ivangorod (at one time the Estonian town of Jaanilinn), on the opposite bank of the River Narva, for centuries.

Narva loss (Narva Castle) also provides the stage for cultural performances, boasts a statue of Lenin (a rare acknowledgement of Estonia's Soviet past) and houses the **Narva muuseum** (Narva Museum). The **Põhjaõu** (Northern Yard) takes visitors back to the 16th and 17th centuries, with an old blacksmith's and pottery.

Those with a head for heights should climb **Pikk Hermann** (Hermann's Tower) and soak up the bird's-eye view over the town, river and **Ivangorod loss** (Ivangorod Castle).

Narva-Jõesuu

Literally translated as the 'mouth of the River Narva', **Narva-Jõesuu** is a coastal resort situated close to the Russian border. During its 19th-century heyday Narva-Jõesuu was renowned as a spa town, attracting wealthy patrons from St Petersburg just 150km (93 miles) away. The resort's attractions are the same – a 7km (4-mile) white sand beach backed by voluminous dunes and fragrant pine trees, plus tranquil parks and a relaxing spa hotel – but the holiday-makers who visit are predominantly Russians living in this part of northeastern Estonia.

WEST COAST

Estonia's pretty west coast boasts the country's premier seaside resorts, Pärnu and Haapsalu, both historic towns brimming with attractions. Elsewhere, tranquil island paradises and pristine sandy beaches like those at **Kakumäe**, **Vääna-Jõesuu** and **Lohusalu** are amongst its biggest drawcards.

Haapsalu **

Balmy sea water, an attractive seaside promenade and curative mud have ensured Haapsalu's popularity with Estonian holiday-makers over the decades. For foreign visitors **Haapsalu loss** (Haapsalu Episcopal Castle) and **Toom-Niguliste kirik** (St Nicholas Dome Church), one of Estonia's best-preserved and most integral cathedrals, are this 13th-century town's principal reasons for visiting. More than a historic relic, the castle is still used for outdoor events.

Other noteworthy buildings include the **Läänemaa muuseum** (Läänemaa Museum, formerly the 18th-century Town Hall), **Jaani kirik** (St John's Church) and the handsome **railway station** (complete in 1907), home to the **Eesti muuseumraudtee** (Estonian Railway Museum). Open Tuesday–Sunday 11:00–17:00.

Pärnu ★★★

Sandy beaches and a lively nightlife (in season) have helped establish **Pärnu** as Estonia's main seaside resort. Pavement cafés, decent restaurants and increasingly sophisticated hotels back up its tourist industry. Whatever the season this old Hanseatic city is also popular with people seeking curative spa therapies (something that it has been offering since the first facility opened in 1838) or just an indulgent massage.

Pärnu's spas have raised the bar in recent years, shedding the old, rough Soviet-style service without a smile in favour of grand refurbishments, polite efficiency and increasingly modern facilities. This is helping the city return to the heydays of the 1930s.

A city whose history can be traced back over 11,000 years, there is more to Pärnu than beaches and spa hotels. Downtown highlights include the Classical **Raekoda** (Town Hall); the Baroque masterpiece that is **Ekateriina kirik** (St Catherine's Church) – built in 1764 it became a template for Orthodox churches throughout the Baltic States; the **Issandamuutmise kirik** (Transfiguration of The Lord Orthodox Church), finished in 1904; and neo-Gothic **Eliisabeti kirik** (Elizabeth Church).

Several important monuments and fortifications also dot Pärnu, with the former prison tower (the **Punane torn** or Red Tower) which forms part of the 15th-century town walls, the 17th-century **Tallinna värav** (Tallinn Gate) and the **Munamägi** defensive bastions being amongst the most impressive.

ISLANDS

Saaremaa ★★★

Lying just south of Hiiumaa, **Saaremaa** is Estonia's largest island. Key sights include the **Angla tuulikud** (Angla Windmills); they may be the only surviving cluster of windmills on the island, but at one time these could be found outside every village.

Elsewhere, the **Kaali kraater** (Kaali Crater), now a circular lake created almost 3000 years ago, and **Vilsandi rahvuspark** (Vilsandi National Park) also merit a visit. Driving around Saaremaa you will also come across appealing churches,

17th- and 18th-century manor houses, forests, ancient and ruined fortifications, attractive bays, lakes, sheer cliff faces, sacrificial springs, lighthouses and nature reserves. Ornithologists will want to visit the lookout tower at **Kogi bog**, a wetland area spanning 40km² (15.5 sq miles).

The main settlement on Saaremaa, **Kuressaare**, also boasts a number of interesting sights. The most important of these is the grand, medieval **Piiskopilinnus** (Bishop's Castle), an art gallery (located in the town hall), and the **Saaremaa muuseum** (Saaremaa Museum). Kuressaare is also home to **Aavik's museum**, which commemorates the life of linguist Johannes Aavik (1880–1973) and his composer cousin Joosep Aavik (1899–1989), and the **Haamers' House Museum**, the home of three brothers who were celebrated locally as an engineer, pastor and painter. Other historic buildings include **Laurentiuse kirik** (St Laurence's Church) and the **law court**.

Muhu *

Linked to its larger sibling by a road bridge, **Muhu** also boasts an old working wooden windmill, **Eemu tuulik** (Eemu Windmill), an absorbing collection of late 19th-century buildings, which comprise the **Muhu muuseum** (Muhu Museum), old churches and fortresses, as well dramatic cliffs.

Hiiumaa *

An island that has yet to embrace the 21st century, it is **Hiiumaa**'s unspoiled nature and unhurried pace of life that attracts holiday-makers. From the 13th-century church at **Pühalepa** (Hiiumaa's oldest) and a couple of handsome lighthouses to the faded grandeur of **Suuremõisa mõis** (Suuremõisa Manor) and the **Hiiumaa muuseum** (Hiiumaa Museum) just outside **Kassari**, the island does have a number of sights. Most visitors, however, come to watch the birds at the **Küina Bay** sanctuary, to soak up the coastal views, or to simply walk and cycle on this peaceful island.

Below: *Windmills are common on the Estonian islands and there are a number of well-preserved wooden mills still standing on Saaremaa.*

Coastal Estonia at a Glance

The Estonian coast is at is busiest during the warm **summer** months, when a largely domestic clientele descends upon its beach resorts and islands. Historic cities like Pärnu and Haapsalu are good places to visit any time.

Rail: Trains run between Pärnu and Tallinn. **Road:** Buses link Haapsalu, Kuressaare and Pärnu to Tallinn, as well as Pärnu and Kuressaare. **Sea:** Ferries run from Rohküla to Heltermaa on Hiiumaa. They also make the crossing between Virtsu and Kuivastu for the islands of Muhu and Saaremaa. **Air:** Seasonal flights operate between Pärnu and Kuressaare on Saaremaa; these stop off on Ruhnu.

The historic hearts of the towns and cities in this chapter can easily be explored on **foot**. **Buses, taxis** and **hire cars** are other ways of getting around.

LUXURY
Victoria Hotel, Kuninga 25, Pärnu, tel: 444 3412, fax: 444 3415, www.victoriahotel.ee This 23-room boutique hotel is housed in an elegant 1920s building. Guests can enjoy drinks in the lobby bar and dinner in the period restaurant, plus wireless Internet access.
Rannahotell, Ranna pst 5,

Pärnu, tel: 443 2950, fax: 443 2918, www.scandic-hotels.com/rannahotell Great views, comfortable rooms and an attractive exterior. Popular with leisure and business guests. It has an on-site restaurant, meeting rooms and salon offering massages.
Spa Hotel Laine, Sadama 9/11, Haapsalu, tel: 472 4400, fax: 272 4401, www.laine.ee Possibly Haapsalu's most contemporary hotel, this luxurious waterfront spa property has modern rooms, a relaxing beauty and massage centre, a 20m pool and one of the town's best restaurants.
Parkhotell Palmse, Lääne-Virumaa, tel: 322 3626, fax: 323 4167, www.phpalmse.ee Stay in one of the 27 modern rooms at the converted distillery of the 18th-century Palmse Manor (see page 108). A fantastic location at the heart of Lahemaa National Park.

MID-RANGE
Grand Rose Spa Hotel, Tallinna 15, Saaremaa, tel: 666 7000, fax: 463 6546, www.grandrose.ee Modern spa hotel in Kuressaare. Elegant rooms and a restaurant.
Kongo Hotel, Kalda 19, Haapsalu, tel: 472 4800, fax: 472 4832, www.kongohotel.ee Welcoming 21-room hotel at the centre of the Old Town with a sauna and restaurant.
Baltic Hotel Promenaadi, Sadama 22, Haapsalu, tel: 473 7250, fax: 473 7254,

www.promenaadi.ee Many of the 35 rooms at this waterfront hotel have balconies and sea views. Single, double and family rooms available.
Hotell Liilia, Hiiu mnt. 22, tel: 463 6146, fax: 463 6546, www.liiliahotell.ee Attractive 13-room hotel in the village of Käina with restaurant and bar.

BUDGET
Narva Hotell, Puškini 6, Narva, tel: 359 9600, fax: 359 9603, www.narvahotell.ee Boxy but modern, central location and reasonable rates.
Tuule B&B, Tuule 2, Paldiski, tel: 679 8123, fax: 514 5116, www.tuule.ee Simple, modern rooms with prices to match. Its five rooms often sell out in advance, so book ahead.
Baltic Country Holidays, Kuģu 11, Riga, tel: 761 7600, fax: 783 0041, www.traveller.lv Agency organizing accommodation in rural Estonia.
SYG Hostel, Kingu 6, Saaremaa, tel: 455 4388. Budget accommodation in Kuressaare.

Valge Laev (Rae 32, Paldiski, tel: 674 2035). As close to British pub grub as you're likely to get in this part of Estonia. Good food.
Café Grand (see Victoria Hotel, Pärnu). Foie gras, black caviar and beef tenderloin feature at this fine-dining restaurant, which has been restored to its original 1920s style.
Blu Holm (see Spa Hotel

Coastal Estonia at a Glance

Laine). Sea views, mouth-watering fish dishes and tasty desserts. One of Haapsalu's best restaurants.

Baltic Hotel Promenaadi (see Baltic Hotel Promenaadi). Sea views and a tempting menu featuring a high percentage of fish dishes. Salads, pasta and grilled meats are also available.

Rannakohvik, Ranna pst 1d, Pärnu, tel: 446 4890, www.kohving.ee This futuristic looking beach café is justifiably popular with the summer crowds who flock here for a sun downer or to enjoy a tasty meal.

SHOPPING

It may not be on a par with Tallinn, but Pärnu is your best bet for those forgotten essentials and holiday souvenirs. For handmade linen pop into Linamaja (Rüütli 37) or Hansa Lina (Ringi 7). The aptly named Suveniir is also located on Ringi. Pärnu also boasts a handful of shopping centres, supermarkets and markets. You will even find a branch of Espirit (Rüütli 45) amongst the city's fashion boutiques.

SPAS

For a rejuvenating break check out one of Pärnu's Spa hotels. These include the Estonian Spa Hotel (www.spaestonia.ee), the Sõprus Spa Hotel (www.spahotelsoprus.com), the

Tervis Spa Hotel (www.spa.ee), the Viiking Spa Hotel (www.viiking.ee) and the Tervise Paradiis Spa Hotel and Water Park (www.spa.ee). For day treatments check out Pärnu's famous Mud Baths or the Estonia Health Rehabilitation Centre. Haapsalu and Saaremaa also have budding spa industries, with the Fra Mare Spa (www.framare.com) and the Grand Rose Spa Hotel both good options.

TOURS AND EXCURSIONS

It is possible to visit Paldiski, Pärnu, Haapsalu, Lahemaa National Park, Muhu, Saaremaa and Hiiumaa on an organized day trip (by coach) from Tallinn. Tiit Reisid is one company offering a variety of excursions around the coast. Agencies running similar tours include Atletikline and Bona Reisid. The same tour operators also run a variety of trips into the Estonian hinterland.

USEFUL CONTACTS

Paldiski Tourist Information, Sadama 9, tel: 679 000, www.paldiski.ee

Narva Tourist Information, Puškini 13, tel: 356 0184, www.narva.ee
Haapsalu Tourist Information, Posti 37, tel: 473 3248, www.haapsalu.ee
Pärnu Tourist Information, Rüütli 16, tel: 447 3000, www.visitparnu.com
Kuressaare Tourist Information, Tallinna 2, tel: 453 3120, www.kuressaare.ee
Muhu Tourist Information, www.muhu.info
Hiiumaa Tourist Information, Hiiu 1, Kärdla, tel: 462 232, www.hiiumaa.ee
Ruhnu Tourist Information, www.ruhnu.ee
Lahemaa National Park, Palmse, tel: 329 5555, www.lahemaa.ee
Vilsandi National Park, www.vilsandi.ee
Tiit Reisid, Tatari 6, Tallinn, tel: 662 3762, www.tiitreisid.ee
Tiit Reisid, Sadama 13, Kärdla, Hiiumaa, tel: 463 2077, fax: 463 2065, www.tiitreisid.ee
Atletikline, Pallasti 12-29, Tallinn, tel: 5552 6113, www.atletikline.ee
Bona Reisid, Estonia pst 1/3, Tallinn, tel: 630 6670, www.bonareisid.ee

PÄRNU	J	F	M	A	M	J	J	A	S	O	N	D
AVERAGE TEMP. °C	-7	-7	-2	3	10	15	17	16	11	5	-1	-5
AVERAGE TEMP. °F	19	19	28	37	50	59	62	60	51	41	30	23
RAINFALL mm	47	31	40	42	39	53	72	74	68	73	79	64
RAINFALL in	1.9	1.2	1.6	1.6	1.5	2.1	2.8	2.9	2.7	2.9	3.1	2.5
DAYS OF RAINFALL	19	18	15	14	11	13	12	15	17	17	20	22

10
Inland Estonia

Break away from the increasingly slick modern face of the Estonian capital and an altogether different Estonia starts to appear. Gone are the gleaming new office blocks and the smooth business hotels and in their place are old wooden houses, crumbling castle ruins and sweeping lakes as the centuries seem to creep back at every turn.

The biggest settlement inland is **Tartu**, a bustling student city that comes as something of a surprise after the swathes of countryside between it and Tallinn. The second largest city in the country boasts a lovely old core and is a good base for exploring inland. Other regional centres worthy of note include **Paide** and **Viljandi**, the latter boasting an atmospheric castle, museums and a lake. **Rakvere** is another highlight with a castle of its own, as well as a sprinkling of museums.

Inland Estonia is teeming with lakes and it also boasts what is Europe's fourth largest lake, **Lake Peipsi**. The lake is shared with Russia and the Russian influence comes through strongly in this eastern part of Estonia. Other natural highlights include the rolling hills around **Otepää**, which come alive in the winter months as part of Estonia's small but fun ski industry. Then there are the protected reserves of the **Karula National Park** and the **Soomaa National Park**, where you really feel as if you are getting away from it all. The former is the smallest national park in the country, whilst the latter is a real wilderness where wolves still roam wild.

DON'T MISS

*** Tartu: home to Estonia's oldest university, a host of other historic buildings and a lively student-orientated nightlife.
** Soomaa National Park: view Estonia's pristine nature.
** Väike-Maarja: historic fortifications and an informative museum. A must.
** Karula National Park: the place for picking (safely) mushrooms and berries.
** Lake Võrtsjärv: enjoy a pleasure cruise aboard an old fishing trawler on Estonia's second largest lake.
** Lake Peipsi: Estonia's biggest lake.

Opposite: *Lake Võrtsjärv is one of the country's most attractive lakes.*

Inland Estonia

Rakvere *

Founded in 1252, Rakvere boasts two well-known sights in its partially ruined medieval **Rakvere linnus** (Rakvere Castle) and the Tarvas statue. The work of Estonian sculptor Tauno Kangro, the latter is an oversized auroch (European bison), which the city proudly proclaims is the largest statue of an animal in the Baltic States.

In addition to its castle museum, the town is also home to a striking Orthodox church, a Lutheran church, two additional museums – **Rakvere linnakodaniku majamuuseum** (Rakvere Citizen's Musuem), an old wooden house whose interior sheds light on early 20th-century life in the city, and **Rakvere näitusemaja** (Rakvere Exhibition House), which has served as a bank and prison since its construction towards the end of the 18th century – and an art gallery, the **Rakvere galerija** (Rakvere Gallery).

Väike-Maarja **

Culturally rich **Väike-Maarja** is a worthwhile diversion. Located in a former schoolhouse (constructed in 1869), the **Väike-Maarja muuseum** (Väike-Maarja Museum) focuses on local history, daily life and the awakening of a national consciousness in the region. The sections that cover the long decades of Soviet rule are perhaps the most interesting, with deportations to Siberia and the community's need to run a collective farm both covered.

Kiltsi loos (Kiltsi Castle) is a striking Baltic-German manor estate dating from the late 18th century. Built in an early Classical style, the mansion was a private home until 1920 when it became a local primary school. An ongoing restoration programme is gradually returning Kiltsi to its original splendour.

The **Vao tornlinnus-muuseum** (Vao Stronghold Tower Museum) harks back to the early 14th century, when medieval fortifications like this dotted Estonia. Originally lookout towers, they soon became important tools for landowners protecting themselves against peasant up-risings. Few of these towers survive, and this one is in par-ticularly good condition.

CENTRAL ESTONIA
Türi
Located at the hub of Estonia's rail network, **Türi** has the dual attractions of pretty public gardens (in spring) and the **Türi muuseum** (Türi Museum), which celebrates the city's industrial development and has a lot of artefacts specifically relating to the railway. Anyone with a passing interest in TV and radio can also visit the **Eesti ringhäälingumuuseum** (Estonian Broadcasting Museum), housed in the same build-ing. Both open Tuesday–Saturday 10:00–17:00.

Paide *
If you are looking for somewhere to stop off between Tallinn and Tartu, then the market town of Paide is a good bet. Its ruined castle, dating from 1265, and the octagonal defence tower, **Pikk Hermann** (Hermann Tower, open Wednesday–Sunday 10:00–18:00), are the main attrac-tions. Both are made from local white limestone. The latter is actually a 1993 reconstruction, as the original was destroyed by the Soviets in 1941; it also provides panoramic views over the surrounding countryside.

Opened in 1905, the **Järvamaa muuseum** (Järvamaa Museum) documents life in the Paide of old through the recreation of a chemist's shop, a room from a manor house and a 1960s apartment and workshops. Open Wednesday–Sunday 11:00–18:00.

GETTING ACTIVE IN SOOMAA NATIONAL PARK

Soomaa National Park is more than just an attractive wetland habitat, it is also a great place to get active outdoors. In a region where dugout canoes were the traditional method of transport for those living in the reserve, one of the most popu-lar activities is canoeing. A more unusual take on this combines kayaking with bog walking. Other activities avail-able in Soomaa include (in winter) ice-fishing, cross-country skiing and snowshoe-ing. For more information visit: www.soomaa.com

TARTU'S BEST MUSEUMS

Gen up on Tartu's early history at the **City Museum**, or learn about Estonia's unique **geology** at the eponymous museum. If you've got a penchant for stuffed animals then the **Museum of Zoology** fits the bill, while the **Literature Museum** houses works by Lydia Koidula (see page 27) and F R Kreutzwald (see page 120). Head back to the bad old days at the **KGB Cells** (formerly the headquarters of the feared Soviet secret police).

PÜHAJÄRV BEACH PARTY FESTIVAL

Not content with being a popular winter sports destination and a relaxed venue for hiking and cycling in the summer, Otepää has also carved out a niche for itself as a lively festival destination. In June each year an international music festival, the Pühajärv Beach Party, graces the shores of its Holy Lake. The crowd may be largely Estonian, but the event does attract others from around the globe.

Viljandi *

Despite a turbulent history that has seen it ravaged by the Russian, German, Swedish and Polish armies over the centuries and various fires destroying many of its old wooden buildings, **Viljandi** still has a number of interesting sights. The most obvious is the crumbling 13th-century **Livonian Order Castle** that dominates the city. The ruins are still integral to local life, with open-air theatre performances and folk music gracing an outdoor stage in the warmer months. The castle also opens up a panoramic view over **Lake Viljandi**.

An 18th-century town hall, neo-Renaissance courthouse, suspension bridge and water tower all number amongst Viljandi's other attractions. Then there is the **Viljandi muuseum** (Viljandi Museum), the neo-Renaissance **Viljandi mõis** (Viljandi Manor) and a couple of handsome churches. Located in an old 18th-century pharmacy, the museum looks at various aspects of local life, including natural history and excavations at the castle. Open Wednesday–Sunday 10:00–17:00.

Lake Võrtsjärv **

Estonia's second largest lake, **Võrtsjärv** (Lake Võrtsjärv), has a surface area of 271km² (105 sq miles) and a maximum depth of 6m (20ft). At one time around 70 traditional wooden trawlers (*kale*) plied the waters of the lake, although they became obsolete when a trawling ban was introduced. Today the reconstructed kaleship *Paula* runs pleasure cruises and fishing trips on Võrtsjärv.

EASTERN ESTONIA
Tartu ***

This vibrant university city, home to more than 15,000 students, is the second largest in Estonia, and well worth a visit. Habitation of the area has been traced back to the 6th century AD, although **Tartu** didn't appear in written records until 1030. In the centuries since it has been ruled by German, Russian, Polish, Lithuanian and Swedish occupiers.

Tartu has long been a centre of education, with the first printing house opening in the city in 1631, followed by the university, under Swedish king Gustavus II Adolphus, in 1632. The city became home to the first teacher-training college in 1684, and perhaps unsurprisingly it was also at the centre of the Estonian national awakening in the latter half of the 19th century.

Tartu's myriad tourist sights include the central **Raekoja plats** (Town Hall Square), which is flanked by handsome 18th- and 20th-century buildings, including the landmark **Raekoda** (Town Hall). Other examples of Tartu's striking architecture include the main neoclassical university building, and the elaborate façade of the restored Gothic **Jaani kirik** (St John's Church). In addition to historic buildings, Tartu, in keeping with its cultural and educational traditions, also boasts well over a dozen museums.

FESTIVALS IN ESTONIA

April • Jazzkaar, Tallinn
(www.jazzkaar.ee)
June–July • **International Student Song and Dance Festival, Tartu**
July • **Early Music Festival, Haapsalu**
July • **Viljandi Folk Music Festival**
(www.folk.ee)
June–August • **Summer Music Festival, Tartu**
November–December **Dark Nights Film Festival, Tallinn**
(www.poff.ee)

Lake Peipsi **

The biggest lake in Estonia and the fourth largest body of water in Europe, **Peipsi järv** (Lake Peipsi) is actually located in both Estonia and the Russian Federation. The latter owns the greater share (56%). Relatively undisturbed by tourism (even Estonians don't really come here), the surface area of the lake is a whopping 3555km^2 (1373 sq miles) and those who make the effort to visit are rewarded by tranquil woodland and quiet sandy beaches. Winter transforms the warm bathing waters into an icy wonderland.

Historically a haven for Old Believers (Russians whose faith was distinct from that of the Orthodox church), many of the villages around the lake have both Lutheran and Orthodox churches. With surprisingly little integration between the Estonian and Russian populations, settlements also tend to be either Estonian or Russian-speaking.

Below: *The ruins of Tartu's cathedral lie on a hill tucked above the centre of this busy university city.*

SOUTHERN ESTONIA

Võru

A good base for anyone who wants to go walking or skiing in the Estonian hills, **Võru** is also home to two decent museums, the **Dr F R Kreuzwaldi memoriaalmuuseum** (F R Kreutzwald Memorial Museum), dedicated to the life and work of a local doctor-cum-poet (open Wednesday–Sunday 10:00–18:00 April–September; Wednesday–Sunday 10:00–17:00 October–March), and the **Võrumaa muuseum** (Võru Regional Museum), which covers the 1918–20 War of Independence and the role of the Forest Brothers particularly well (open Wednesday–Sunday 11:00–18:00).

Obinitsa

At the heart of **Setumaa** and Estonia's distinctive **Setu** culture, **Obinitsa** itself boasts the **Seto muuseumitaro Obinitsa** (Setu Museum Obinitsa, open 10:00–17:00). In the vicinity you will also find the **Seto talumuuseum** (Setu Farm Museum) in Värska. Further examples of Setu culture can be found at Obinitsa's artificial lake, where there is a statue of the Setu Mother of Song, and at another Setu museum in Saatse.

Around 5km (3 miles) from Obinitsa the **Sandstone Caves** in **Piusa** are an interesting diversion. Open daily in summer.

Karula National Park **

Estonia's smallest national park, **Karula**, boasts an attractive landscape of meadow, forest, lakes and bogs. For visitors this translates into a tranquil environment for walking, swimming and fishing, as well as berry/mushroom picking (with a guide).

WESTERN ESTONIA

Soomaa National Park **

Established in 1993 and spanning some 371km^2 (143 sq miles), the landscape of **Soomaa National Park** is characterized by thick forest and flat marshy flood plains and rivers. It is also home to myriad animal and bird species, including beavers, otters, waterfowl, eagles and wolves. It is perhaps not surprising that the importance of this unique wetland is recognized internationally.

Inland Estonia at a Glance

Inland Estonia offers something for every season, from lake swimming in **summer** to skiing in **winter** and hiking and cycling in **spring** or **autumn**.

Rail: Direct services run from Tartu to Tallinn. **Road:** Bus links include those from Tartu to Rakvere and Viljandi.

Many of the towns and cities are navigable on **foot**. **Buses**, **taxis** and **hire cars** are another way of getting around.

Draakon, Raekoja plats 2, Tartu, tel: 744 2045, fax: 742 300, www.draakon.ee Pleasant, comfortable rooms, atmospheric beer cellar and a great Baroque restaurant.
Barclay, Ülikooli 8, Tartu, tel: 744 7100, fax: 744 7110, www.barclay.ee Spacious, in early 20th-century building.
London, Rüütli 9, Tartu, tel: 730 5555, fax: 730 5565, www.londonhotel.ee Light and modern rooms.
Uppsala Maja, Jaani 7, Tartu, tel: 736 1535, fax: 736 1536, www.uppsalamaja.ee Five-star guesthouse in one of Tartu's oldest wooden buildings. Booking essential.
Katariina, Pikk 3, Rakvere, tel: 322 3943, fax: 322 3331, www.katariina.ee 24-room guesthouse on one of Rakvere's oldest streets.

Nelja Kuninga Hotell, Pärnu tn 6, Paide, tel: 385 0882, www.nelikuningat.ee Solid three-star hotel.
Grand Hotel Viljandi, Tartu 11/Lossi 29, Viljandi, tel: 435 5800, fax: 435 5805, www.ghv.ee Elegant 1938 hotel with 48 individually styled rooms, gym and sauna.
Centrum, Tallinna 24, Viljandi, tel: 435 1100, fax: 435 1130, www.centrum.ee Perfectly acceptable three-star with 25 rooms.
Kesklinna Hotell, Lipuväljak 11, Otepää, tel: 765 5095, fax: 766 1229, www.kesk linnahotell.ee Good rates, flexible accommodation (doubles, twins, triples and family suites), sauna and private parking.
Külalistemaja Hermes, Jüri 32a, Võru, tel: 782 1326, www.hotel.ee/hermes Good value, no-frills rooms.

Draakon (see Draakon Hotel, Tartu).
Eesti Restoran (see Barclay Hotel, Tartu). Feast on modern Estonian cuisine.
Grand Hotel Viljandi (see

Grand Hotel Viljandi). International food in stylish surrounds.
Centrum (see Centrum Hotel, Viljandi). One of Viljandi's best restaurants.

Rakvere Tourist Information, Laada 14, tel: 324 2734, www.rakvere.ee
Väike-Maarja Tourist Information, Pikk 3, tel: 326 1625, www.v-maarja.ee
Paide Tourist Information, Keskväljak 14, tel: 383 8600, www.paide.ee
Viljandi Tourist Information, Vabaduse plats 6, tel: 433 0442, www.viljandimaa.ee
Tartu Tourist Information, Raekoja plats 14, tel: 744 2111, www.visittartu.com
Otepää Tourist Information, Tartu mnt 1, tel: 766 1200, www.otepaa.ee
Võru Tourist Information, Tartu tn 31, tel: 782 1881, www.voru.ee
Karula National Park, tel: 782 8350, www.karula rahvuspark.ee
Soomaa National Park, www.soomaa.com
Kaleship Tours, www. vortsjarve.ee

TARTU	J	F	M	A	M	J	J	A	S	O	N	D
AVERAGE TEMP. °C	-5	-6	-1	4	11	15	16	15	10	6	0	-3
AVERAGE TEMP. °F	22	21	30	40	52	59	62	60	51	43	33	25
RAINFALL mm	38	25	33	33	38	51	69	71	69	64	66	51
RAINFALL in	1.5	1.0	1.3	1.3	1.5	2.0	2.7	2.8	2.7	2.5	2.6	2.0
DAYS OF RAINFALL	20	17	16	13	11	13	12	14	16	16	21	23

Travel Tips

Tourist Information

Lithuania

Main overseas offices:

Finland: Kapteeninkatu 7, 00140 Helsinki, tel: (358 9) 6227 7717, fax: (358 9) 6227 7718, email: info@liettua.fi www.liettua.fi

Poland: Al. Ujazdowskie 51, 00-536 Warsaw, tel: (48 22) 584 7052, fax: (48 22) 584 7073, email: info@litwatravel.com www.litwatravel.com

Lithuanian State Department of Tourism: A. Juozapaviãius, Vilnius, tel: (370 5) 210 8796, fax: (370 5) 210 8753, email: info@tourism.lt www.tourism.lt

Latvia

Main overseas offices:

Finland: Mariankatu 8b, FIN-00170, Helsinki, tel: (358 9) 278 4774, fax: (358 9) 6874 2650, email: Helsinki@latviatouris.lv www.latviatourism.lv

UK: 72 Queensborough Terrace, London W2 3SH, tel: (44 20) 7229 8271, fax: (44 20) 7727 7397, email: london@latviatouris.lv www.latviatourism.lv

Latvian Tourism Information Bureau: Smilšu iela 4, Rīga, tel: (371) 6722 4664, fax: (371) 6722 4665, email: info@latviatourism.lv www.latviatourism.lv

Estonia

Main overseas offices:

UK: 6 Hyde Park Gate, London SW7 5DG, tel: (44 020) 7838 5390, fax: (44 020) 7838 5391, email: london@eas.ee www.visitestonia.com

Germany: Mönckebergstr. 5, 20095 Hamburg, tel: (49 40) 3038 7899, fax: (49 40) 3038 7981, email: hamburg@eas.ee www.visitestonia.com

Estonian Tourist Board: Liivalaia 13/15, 10118 Tallinn, tel: (372) 627 9770, fax: (372) 627 9777, email: tourism@aes.ee www.visitestonia.com

Baltic Tourism Information Centre in Germany: Katharinenstr. 19-20, 10711 Berlin-Wilmersdorf, tel: (49 30) 8900 9091, fax: (49 30) 8900 9092, email: info@baltikuminfo.de www.baltikuminfo.de

Entry Requirements

Most visitors, including those from the European Union (EU) and European Economic Area (EEA), only need a valid passport or National Identity card to enter the Baltic States. Current visa regulations can be checked with the relevant Ministry of Foreign Affairs: Lithuania (www.urm.lt), Latvia (www.mfa.gov.lv) and Estonia (www.vm.ee). The Baltic Sates joined the Schengen Zone in December 2007; in principle this allows visitors to pass between countries without border checks.

Customs

Lithuania, Latvia and Estonia are all EU member states; this means that there is no duty-free allowance for those travelling from another EU country. Consumer goods for your own personal use can also be transported freely without incurring additional tax. Some restrictions, however, still apply. Visitors from within the EU are allowed to bring a maximum of 800 cigarettes, 400 cigarillos, 200 cigars, 1kg tobacco, 110 litres of beer, 90 litres of wine, 20 litres of liqueur, 10 litres of spirits, 10 kg of coffee and 110 litres of non-alcoholic beverages. Visitors from outside the EU are permitted to bring 200 cigarettes or the equivalent, one litre of spirits or two litres of liqueur or wine, 50g of perfume, 250ml eau de toilette and new/unused items to the value of € 175 into any of the three Baltic States without paying customs duty.

Health Requirements

You do not need any vaccinations to visit the Baltic States. EU citizens in possession of a European Health Insurance Card (EHIC) are entitled to free emergency health care in the Baltics. Non-emergency treatment, prescriptions and repatriation costs, however, are not covered by the EHIC and all visitors should purchase full travel insurance.

Getting There

Lithuania

By Air: Lithuanian Airlines (www.lal.lt) fly direct from locations across Europe to the international airports at Vilnius (www.vilnius-airport.lt) and Palanga (www.palanga-airport.lt). There is a third international airport at Kaunas (www.kaunasair.lt). Air Baltic (www.airbaltic.com), Czech

Airlines (www.czech airlines.com), Estonian Air (www.estonian-air.ee), Finnair (www.finnair.com) and Lufthansa (www.lufthansa.com) also fly to Vilnius. Ryanair (www.ryanair.com) fly direct to Kaunas.

By Road: International buses (www.eurolines.com) connect Lithuania to its neighbouring countries, as well as other European cities, including Berlin, London, Prague and Rome.

By Rail: Direct international rail services (www.litrail.lt) link Vilnius to Minsk, Moscow, Odessa, St Petersburg and Warsaw. International services also run from Kaunas to Riga and from Klaipėda to both Moscow and St Petersburg.

By Boat: Ferries to Klaipėda run from Århus and Aabenraa in Denmark (www.scand lines.lt), Baltiysk in Kaliningrad (www.lisco.lt), Karlshamn in Sweden (www.lisco.lt) and Kiel and Sassnitz in Germany (www.lisco.lt).

Latvia

By Air: Air Baltic (www.air baltic.com) fly direct from locations across Europe to Riga International Airport (www.Riga-airport.com). Aerlingus (www.aerlingus.com), easyJet (www.easyjet.com), KLM (www.klm.com) and Ryanair (www.ryanair.com) also fly to Riga.

By Road: International buses (www.eurolines.com, www.ecolines.net and

ROAD SIGNS

Road signs in the Baltic States are quite straightforward and should present no real problems to drivers who have not driven in the region before now that Cyrillic is gone. On highways arrows with the destination name indicate which lane you should be in, similar signs are found at major junctions and in some cases a road designation number is also shown. Mandatory speed limits are given inside a circle.

www.nordeka.lv) connect Latvia to destinations throughout Europe.

By Rail: Direct international rail services (www.ldz.lv) run from Riga to Kaunas, Moscow and St Petersburg.

By Boat: Riga is linked by ferry to Stockholm in Sweden (http://pramis.rcc.lv) and Lübeck in Germany (www.dfdstorline.lv). Services also run from Ventspils to Rostock in Germany (www.scandlines.lt) and Nynäsham and Karlsham in Sweden (www.scandlines.lt). From May–September a ferry runs from Ventspils to Saaremaa in Estonia (www.slkferries.ee).

Estonia

By Air: Estonian Air (www.estonian-air.ee) fly direct to Tallinn from destinations throughout Europe. Air Baltic (www.airbaltic.com), Czech Airlines (www.czechairlines.com), easyJet (www.easyjet.com), Finnair (www.finnair.com) and Lufthansa (www.lufthansa.com) also fly to the airport.

By Road: International buses services (www.eurolines.com) run to and from Latvia, as well as to destinations like Hamburg, Kaliningrad, Kiev, Munich and St Petersburg.

By Rail: Direct international rail services (www.erv.ee) link Tallinn to Moscow and St Petersburg.

By Boat: Tallinn can be reached by ferry from Helsinki (Finland), Stockholm (Sweden) and Rostock (Germany). Check the following websites for service details: www.tallink.ee www.eckeroline.ee www.superseacat.com www.vikingline.fi and www.njl.ee

What to Pack

Sun lotion, sunglasses and lightweight clothing are essential summer items. In winter temperatures often plummet below 0°C (32°F), so you'll need warm clothes. Other essentials include camera battery chargers/spare batteries, digital photo memory cards/camera film and plug adaptors. An umbrella or waterproof jacket might be needed at any time of year. It is also a good idea to photocopy important documents and to make a note of any prescription medicines that you are taking. Consider packing spare glasses and contact lenses.

Money Matters

Currency: Lithuania's national currency is the *lita* (LTL), Latvia's is the *lat* (LVL) and Estonia's the Estonia *kroon* (EEK). There are 100 *centų* to the *lita*, 100 *santīmi* to the *lat* and 100 cents to the *kroon*.

Currency Exchange: Cash can be exchanged at banks, hotels, travel agencies and exchange offices throughout the Baltic States. Traveller's cheques can also be changed in banks and some travel agencies.

Credit Cards: Maestro, Mastercard, Visa, Cirrus and American Express are commonly accepted.

Tipping: Some restaurants automatically levy a 10% service charge. Where no service charge is indicated it is courteous to leave a 10–15% tip.

VAT: The standard rate of Value Added Tax is 18%.

Accommodation

The Baltic States have accommodation to suit every budget from camp sites, private rooms and hostels to large business hotels and five-star boutique hotels. Properties increasingly have their own websites, which can be useful when you want to make an advance booking.

Eating Out

Cafés, snack bars, fast-food joints, traditional inns and restaurants cater to a wide range of budgets. Myriad international cuisines are available in Vilnius, Rīga and Tallinn.

Transport
Lithuania

Road: The quality of Lithuania's roads varies widely from rough muddy tracks to new tarmac highways. To hire a car you must be at least 21 years old and have held a full and valid driving licence for one to two years. You will need a passport and credit card to secure the rental. Country maps are usually included as part of the hire. If you are stopped by the police they will ask to see your passport/national ID card and

---

CONVERSION CHART

From	To	Multiply By
Millimetres	Inches	0.0394
Metres	Yards	1.0936
Metres	Feet	3.281
Kilometres	Miles	0.6214
Square kilometres	Square miles	0.386
Hectares	Acres	2.471
Litres	Pints	1.760
Kilograms	Pounds	2.205
Tonnes	Tons	0.984
To convert Celsius to Fahrenheit: x 9 ÷ 5 + 32		

driving licence, as well as the car's registration and insurance documents.

If you are driving your own car you will need a Green Card (international vehicle insurance). The basic rules are as follows: drive on the right, seat belts are compulsory, keep headlights turned on, blood alcohol must not be more than 0.04%, do not exceed 50kmph in towns, 90kmph on highways or 110kmph on dual carriageways. In the event of an accident contact the police (tel: 02).

The Association of Lithuanian Automobilists (LAS) provide roadside assistance: tel: 1888 or 1414 (from a mobile phone) or 8 8000 0000 (from a landline).

Buses: Lithuania has a good network of local and long-distance coaches, with frequent departures and reasonable journey times.

Trains: Lithuania's train stock is dated and journeys are often slow and indirect. Lithuanian Railways, www.litrail.lt

Trolleybuses: Vilnius and Kaunas have a trolleybus network.

Latvia
Air: Air Baltic (www.air baltic.com) operate internal flights between Rīga and Liepāja.

Road: As in Lithuania, the quality of Latvia's roads varies. The conditions for hiring a car and the rules of the road are almost the same. The driver's blood alcohol limit must be below 0.05% and speed on dual carriageways should not exceed 100kmph. In the event of a breakdown contact the Latvian Automobile Association (tel: 1888).

Buses: Latvia has comprehensive local and long-distance bus networks.

Trains: For tourists the most useful national train routes connect Rīga to Jūrmala, Jelgava and Sigulda. Latvian Railways (tel: 1181, www.ldz.lv).

Trolleybuses/Trams: Trolleybuses and trams, which use the same tickets as the local buses, also operate in Rīga.

Estonia
Road: Car rental conditions are the same as those for Lithuania. Driving is on the right, seat belts are compulsory, headlights must be turned on at all times, blood alcohol must not exceed 0.02%, the speed limit is 50kmph in towns and 90kmph on highways. The Automobile Club of Estonia, tel: 1888, provide roadside assistance.

Buses: Tallin has an efficient bus network. Tickets for national and international routes can be purchased at local bus stations.

Trains: Edelaraudette (www.edel.ee) operate intercity services. Elektriraudtee (www.elektriraudtee.ee) run local electric trains.

Trolleybuses/Trams: Trolleybuses and trams, which use the same tickets as the local buses, also operate in Tallinn.

Business Hours
Office Hours: Monday–Friday 09:00–18:00.

Post Offices: Monday–Friday 08:00–18:00 (some open later and on Saturdays).

Banks: Monday–Friday 09:00–18:00 (some open on Saturdays).

Time Difference
GMT +2 hours.

Communications
Lithuania
Post: Lietuvos Paštas (www.post.lt) operate Lithuania's postal service. Post office services include postage, fax, credit card cash advances and photocopying.

Telephone: You can make a direct local, national or international call from any public telephone in Lithuania; these require a phone card (sold at newspaper kiosks). When placing a local call omit the area code. If calling from overseas dial the country code (+370) and the area code. Confusingly a new system has been introduced for making national calls, with the caller needing to dial an 8 before the area code. If you are planning to use your mobile, consider buying a prepaid call card from the local GSM service providers Bite (www.bite.lt), Omitel (www.omnitel.lt) or Tele2 (www.tele2.lt).

Fax: You can send and receive faxes in the majority of Lithuania's expensive hotels, as well as at some post offices.

Internet cafés: Tourist offices in larger towns and cities should be able to point you in the direction of the nearest public Internet terminal.

Latvia

Post: Latvijas Pasts (www.pasts.lv) operate Latvia's postal service. Additional services in larger branches include currency exchange and international calls.

Telephone: You can make a direct local, national or international call from any public telephone using a *telekarte* (phone card) sold at newspaper kiosks, post offices and shops displaying the *telekarte* sign. There are no area codes. Country code is +371. Prepaid mobile phone cards are available from Latvijas Mobilais Telefons (www.lmt.lv).

Fax: More expensive hotels will often be able to send/receive faxes on your behalf.

Internet cafés: Tourist offices in larger towns and cities will have information about public Internet access.

Estonia

Post: Eesti Post (www.post.ee) operate Estonia's postal service with regular, express and courier delivery options. Some branches can also arrange Western Union international money orders.

Telephone: You can make a direct local, national or international call from any public telephone using a phone card (available from post offices and newspaper kiosks). There are no area codes. Country code is +372. Prepaid mobile phone cards are available

from AS EMT (www.emt.ee), Elisa (www.elisa.ee) and Tele2 (www.tele2.ee).

Fax: Most up-market hotels will send/receive faxes.

Internet cafés: Ask locally for the nearest Internet café.

Electricity

220 volts, 50 AC. European two-pin round-pronged plugs.

Weights and Measures

The Baltic States use the metric system.

Health Precautions

You do not need to take any special health precautions when travelling to the Baltic States. In summer protect against the sun with sunscreen, sunglasses and a hat; you should also drink plenty of water to avoid dehydration. Tap water is safe to drink. Precautions should also be taken against sexually transmitted diseases.

Health Services

You will find a hospital or medical centre in all main towns and cities in the Baltic States, as well as a pharmacy. Hotels and other accommodation establishments often keep the number of a 24-hour doctor or pharmacy.

Personal Safety

Each of the Baltic States experiences its fair share of petty and more serious crime. Simple precautions like carrying your valuables securely and out of sight (the same applies to valuables in vehicles) should help

Good Reading

O'Connor, Kevin, *The History of the Baltic States*, Greenwood Press, Burnham (2003).
Lieven, Anatol, *The Baltic Revolution: Estonia, Latvia, Lithuania and the Path to Independence*, Yale University Press, London (1996).
Smith, David, *The Baltic States: Estonia, Latvia and Lithuania*, Routledge, Abingdon (2002).
Mole, Richard, *The Baltic States: From Soviet Union to European Union*, Routledge, Abingdon (2008).

keep you safe. Drunken men, in particular, also fall prey to crime (robbery and assault), so consume alcohol in moderation. Avoid walking alone in dark and secluded spaces. If a crime is committed against you, report it to the police immediately.

Emergencies

Emergency calls in Lithuania and Latvia: fire 01, police 02 and ambulance 03 (all 112 from a mobile phone). In Estonia dial 112 for fire or ambulance and 110 for police.

Language

Lithuanian is a Baltic language. Latvian is also a Baltic language, with similar vocabulary and grammar to Lithuanian; the pronunciation, though, is different. Estonian is a Finno-Ugric language that has more in common with Finnish than that of its Baltic State neighbours.